EDITED BY  ...RI
SERIES EDIT... BENNETT

THE research ⟟ED GUIDE TO

ASSESSMENT

....

AN EVIDENCE-INFORMED GUIDE FOR TEACHERS

First Published 2020

by John Catt Educational Ltd,
15 Riduna Park, Station Road,
Melton, Woodbridge IP12 1QT

Tel: +44 (0) 1394 389850
Email: enquiries@johncatt.com
Website: www.johncatt.com

ISBN: 978 1 913622 13 8

Set and designed by John Catt Educational Limited

WHAT IS researchED?

researchED is an international, grassroots education-improvement movement that was founded in 2013 by Tom Bennett, a London-based high school teacher and author. researchED is a truly unique, teacher-led phenomenon, bringing people from all areas of education together onto a level playing field. Speakers include teachers, principals, professor, researchers and policy makers.

Since our first sell-out event, researchED has spread all across the UK, into the Netherlands, Norway, Sweden, Australia, the USA, with events planned in Spain, Japan, South Africa and more. We hold general days as well as themed events, such as researchED Maths & Science, or researchED Tech.

WHO ARE WE?

Since 2013, researchED has grown from a tweet to an international conference movement that so far has spanned six continents and thirteen countries. We have simple aims: to help teaching become more evidence-facing; to raise the research literacy in teaching; to improve education research standards; and to bring research users and research creators closer together. To do this, we hold unique one-day conferences that bring together teachers, researchers, academics and anyone touched by research. We believe in teacher voice, and short-circuiting the top-down approach to education that benefits no one.

HOW DOES IT WORK?

The gathering of mainly teachers, researchers, school leaders, policymakers and edu-bloggers creates a unique dynamic. Teachers and researchers can attend the sessions all day and engage with each other to exchange ideas. The vast majority of speakers stay for the duration of the conference, visit each other's sessions, work on the expansion of their knowledge and gain a deeper understanding of the work of their peers. Teachers can take note of recent developments in educational research, but are also given the opportunity to provide feedback on the applicability of research or practical obstacles.

CONTENTS

FOREWORD

BY TOM BENNETT

Is there an area of education more over simplified in the minds of non-practitioners than assessment? Teaching embodies the Dunning-Kruger effect in the minds of the laity everywhere. Most people have sat glumly in a classroom, which leads many to an illusory grasp of wisdom in its practice, a syndrome that would worry us more if people felt the same way about flying a plane or keyhole surgery. The non-teacher looks at a matter like assessment and thinks, 'How hard can that be?' Instinctively it seems no more complex than checking the student's responses against a bank of incontrovertibly correct answers and following the mark scheme. Turn the handle and – voila! – out comes the grade like a sausage.

Five minutes in a classroom actually trying to do it should be enough to disarm you of this fairy tale. I remember my own clown-car experience of learning to grade essays. Two weeks into my first placement and I was asked by my mentor if I wanted to mark some exam scripts. Boy, did I ever! She handed me a scrap of paper that looked as though a bag of mice had scurried through a pool of ink and across an exercise book. 'What would you give that one?' she said, indicating a short response.

I looked at the sentence. 'I have no idea,' I said.
'Well, is it one mark, two marks, whatever?'
'I don't even know how many marks it's out of,' I said.
'It's out of four,' she replied impatiently. 'What would you give it?' I read the question and looked at the answer.
'I don't know,' I said. 'How much detail are they supposed to give?'
'Look, just give it a mark.' This seemed quite mad. What on earth was the benchmark for each mark? But I was brand new.
'Er, I'd give it zero,' I said.
'Why?'
'Because the question asks "Why might a Muslim not agree with divorce?" and they've written "Because they don't believe in it." That's not really answering the question, is it? Also they spelled every word wrong, including 'it', which is quite impressive.'

'No,' she said, sounding annoyed. 'It's one mark.'

'But why should it get any mark?' I said.

'Because with these kids, you have to look for marks. It's not just what they write; it's what you think they mean. He probably means that the Qur'an teaches that it is accepted but not encouraged.'

'But he didn't *write* that. Do we mark them for what they write or what we think they know?'

'Look, you just have to accept what I'm telling you,' she said, closing the matter. 'Mark these,' and she passed me a pile of these masterpieces.

I kid you not: that was my training. I spent the next two hours pretending to mark them. What I ended up doing was marking them against each other, giving the worst answers (of which the example I just gave you wasn't by any means one) zero, and the best ones full marks (and even with the zeros I was looking for some invisible inky goodness buried inside it, like ghostly treasure).

It turns out that what I was doing was, in the circumstances, probably the best thing I could have made out of a dire situation. I had never been taught how to mark or assess a piece of work in my formal teacher preparation programme. Like most of what constitutes actual teaching, I was expected to 'pick it up as I went along', that old fallback used by Pollyannas everywhere. Looking back, I'm not sure my mentor was taught much about it either. Perhaps her brittle response to my gentle requests for guidance was prompted by the realisation that nobody in that room knew much about marking.

What I didn't realise at the time was that this wasn't a local problem. This wasn't a bug in the teacher training system; this was a feature. Incomprehension was baked into our preparation. The way we were being sent into classroom combat was more akin to the way adolescents are initiated into adulthood by shamans: huff the smoke, look into the eyes of God and know the secrets of the universe, but don't tell anyone what you saw.

We are wading slowly out of this primordial mud, but it is heavy weather. We have made progress in the years since I trained to teach, but it is hard won, and every step forward we slide a few back some days. There is a growing realisation, internationally, that unless we formally teach these processes to teachers, we may as well fling zebras at the kids and hope they learn Pythagoras' theorem from the experience. Teachers are starting to think about what assessment is for, when it is meaningful and when it is not, and how to create our own mark schemes, rubrics and grading methods. Given where we started, at times it has felt like the opening scene in *2001: A Space Odyssey*, where early man discovers tools by smashing his neighbour's head in with a thigh bone.

And if we are making progress, it is because we are starting to think about assessment as an academic process, one subject to scrutiny, dissection and rebuilding. There has been a great and ferocious blossoming of discussion, writing and debate about the moral and practical barriers and opportunities afforded by assessment. And with everything else, evidence has been in the DNA of this resurrection of reason. It has to be, or we go back to guessing alone in the dark, with its hunches, biases and the fear of being found out.

And I hope that researchED as has played a small part of this, as a movement and a community that has tried its best to reach into the classrooms and mind palaces of teachers everywhere. This has been a bottom-up revolution, catching fire in the brush rather than the forest canopy. And this book will, I hope, help continue that process, and become a resource that teachers and educators of all stripes can refer to as they grow and train in their careers. Sarah Donarski has assembled a worthy diet of brilliant thinkers and voices from both academia and the classroom. I commend its digestion to you, like a chef kissing his fingers as he passes the ratatouille from the kitchen to the customer.

Good luck, and love to you all.

Tom Bennett

INTRODUCTION

THE NEED FOR A RESEARCHED MINI-SERIES ON ASSSESSMENT, MARKING AND FEEDBACK

SARAH DONARSKI

A teacher's job, according to Dylan Wiliam (2011), is to create an environment where our students' engagement in learning proceeds towards an intended direction. That is to say that we, as teachers, should not be focusing simply on 'transmitting' knowledge or 'facilitating' learning; we should also be focusing on establishing a classroom ecosystem (to use Tom Sherrington's *Learning Rainforest* metaphor) where teaching and learning becomes fluid yet remains targeted. In order for this to occur, we must form a bridge between the teaching of material in the classroom and how the learning of that information is being processed and manipulated by our students. The only way we can do this effectively, Wiliam astutely claims, is through this process of assessment.

When we look at areas of pedagogy, assessment, marking and feedback are topics that are frequently bulked together, and I would like to start by asking you, your departments, or your colleagues:

- What do assessment, marking and feedback (both separately and collectively) mean to you, your department, and your school?
- What strategies are working or failing in these areas?
- What brings you excitement or anxiety when considering these concepts?

Understanding the answers to these questions will assist in providing clarity on exactly what needs refining, resolving or reconstructing in your context. As we shall see, the recent theoretical history on how to effectively establish and implement these areas of teaching into policy has caused much confusion. However, there is no better time to consider how assessment, marking and feedback have changed over the years so that conversations about how best to move forward can begin.

How did we get here?

Developing effective policies plays an integral part in a school's ability to monitor, track and understand its pupils' progress. Various publications, including the large-scale studies conducted by the Education Endowment Foundation (2018; Elliot et al., 2016), continue to suggest that feedback from assessments is one of the key strategies to assist a student in making progress.

The value of assessment, marking and feedback has also never been ignored by schools, governors, or Ofsted – previously resulting in a range of timely teaching practices. Strategies such as deep written marking and triple marking (until quite recently) became the fashionable mannequins of effective feedback. Unsurprisingly, this resulted in a soaring (yet frighteningly accepted) marking workload until a publication from the Department for Education (2016) claimed that a review of educational literature proved 'there appears to be no broadly agreed definition for this term or any theoretical underpinning of [deep written marking's] educational worth' (p. 6).

The DfE's (2016) report began to spark a different conversation about assessment, marking and feedback, and successfully encouraged many schools to begin the process of augmenting their feedback and assessment policies. Ofsted began to look for curriculum and assessment quality rather than evidence of marking or feedback dialogues. As a result, some schools remained highly attached to timely written marking, whilst others banished it completely in favour of peer, group or verbal feedback approaches. Yet new anxieties emerged: what exactly, and to what extent, should we be assessing or marking? What we should be doing when we plan assessments and how best to deliver feedback to our students remain crucial priorities for many schools, colleges, and educational contexts.

What are the current debates?

Assessments are produced so that teachers can give feedback to students; however, there is a clear misalignment among educational theorists on what exactly feedback or marking are. Kulhavy (1977) argued that feedback is not simply informing a student about what is correct but should instigate a new instruction from the teacher; a task that encourages a pupil's correctional methodology. With similar confidence, Winne and Butler (1994) provide an acknowledged summary of feedback by claiming that it is:

> Information with which a learner can confirm, add to, overwrite, tune, or restructure information in memory, whether that information is domain

knowledge, meta-cognitive knowledge, beliefs about self and tasks, or cognitive tactics and strategies (Winne and Butler, 1994, p. 5740)

However, counter to this is a study conducted by O'Neill et al. (1976) who challenges this theoretical definition by arguing that the 'best immediate retention' (or memory) of answers in feedback was achieved when 'feedback could be given by handing students a key showing all the correct answers'. In this case, feedback was not something that a learner could 'overwrite' (Winne and Butler, 1994, p. 5740) but was something that should be given 'immediate[ly]' and 'without search[ing]' (O'Neill et al., 1976, p. 74). Feedback, according to O'Neill et al. (1976), is giving students the answer. This confusing and debated theoretical discussion has also led to disputing the practical application of marking and feedback, and the style of assessments that departments should be implementing.

In most cases, the commonly accepted method of classroom feedback still considers the teacher to be the primary feedback deliverer. Hattie and Timperley (2007) identify feedback as a teacher's response to an instructed performative task; a secondary process that occurs following a student task. They argue that it is vital in addressing the misconceptions of a student's knowledge base and that it assists to counteract knowledge limitations (Hattie and Timperley, 2007). Why written feedback should be completed by the classroom teacher and not another individual is therefore argued to be due to the teacher's expertise in the subject. According to Gielan et al. (2010), a teacher's background in the subject material is perceived to be more 'trustworthy' and, as a result, appears more effective to the student. Moreover, teachers are not only bringing in their subject knowledge, but their disposition: skills in empathy, compassion and discourse that will most effectively assist a student in moving forward. Teachers have the knowledge set of the task and assessment criterion, enabling their written feedback to 'give [students] insights into various ways to solve the assignments' (Gielan et al., 2010, p. 144). This idea has also been explored by Sadler, who similarly argues that the role of a teacher is to reduce the rate of error in trial–and-error learning; the teacher is responsible for, and accountable to, the learner in this regard (Sadler, 1998).

However, due to bias limitations in assessment, marking and feedback, as well as our continual experimentation with more effectual and less-timely practices, more recent studies question the value of individualised, teacher-led feedback for assessments. A recent small-scale study by Evidence Based Education (Kime, 2018) worked with three schools to change their feedback policies in accordance with the DfE's (2016) report. Of note were the findings from Tarporley High School, where English teachers replaced individual teacher-student marking entirely in favour of group verbal feedback methods using a visualiser (Kime, 2018). The findings on classroom attainment concluded that teachers saved 'roughly 4.3 hours' a week and there was 'virtually no difference' (Kime and Lowe, 2018) in the results of the students using group and verbal feedback methods. In particular, the variance of results between control and tested classes of English pupils were even considered 'too small to be statistically significant' (Kime, 2018, p. 17).

But is 'no difference' in results the same as success? One may argue that this has not entirely made this a successful policy change, and there are still ongoing debates about whether schools are effectively evaluating the limitations of group or verbal feedback. Indeed, the DfE's (2016) report argues that replacing written dialogue with verbal conversations is simply useful in eliminating 'wasted teacher time'. Therefore, perhaps it could be argued that a shift from a written approach to a verbal approach assists teachers but may not impact the progress of all students – in particular, struggling or disengaged pupils. Whatever your perspective, Kime's (2018) study does highlight that there are intricacies and debatable approaches to consider when it comes to delivering effective feedback (verbal or written) to our pupils. It also highlights the ongoing discussion as to whether successful feedback is about time gained and/or the progress of all classroom students (both being the answer we are all searching for in practice).

Yet, there is another solution presented to us. Daisy Christodoulou's endorsement of No More Marking – a technological programme that aims to revolutionise marking through comparative judgement – takes marking and feedback to a new end of the educational debate spectrum. In this process of assessing, work is graded comparatively and, as Christodoulou states, helps with assessment 'reliability, efficiency, and validity' (Christodoulou, 2018, p. 8)

Marking and feedback methods are undoubtedly confused and conflicted, but so too is the issue of when to use them in our classroom. Should peer and group marking be used for 'formative' assessment, and teacher marking for 'summative'? How many pieces of 'formative' or 'summative' assessment should there be in an academic year? I will let some of the chapters in this book answer those questions.

Even after all of this has been considered, there remains contention around whether assessments require a grade or mark and whether there is much validity in that data regardless. The conflict surrounding grade use on summative or formative assessments was instigated by Butler's research which claimed that feedback with grades skewed a student's interest away from learning and progress, moving a student's interest towards 'ego-involvement' and away from 'task involvement' (Butler, 1988, p.10). Butler's study was conclusive that grades in feedback – either solely or attached to comments – undermined lower achievers and, therefore, did not have the greatest effect on all students' progress (Butler, 1988). Correspondingly, McMillan et al.'s (2002) research argues that grading in feedback is incredibly nuanced and biased. In their findings, they noted strong discrepancies between the feedback and grading given within schools and claimed that 'within-school variance' in feedback is greater than 'between-school variance' (McMillan et al., 2002, p. 212). Their data suggests that there are a considerable number of factors that influence the way that a teacher may give feedback and grade a student, including biases towards behaviour, handwriting and/or negative relationships.

Butler's (1988) study should not be ignored entirely and her findings should be noted: there can sometimes be no effective purpose in communicating numerical grades to students if that does not add to, or assist in, the overall purpose of the feedback being given. Consistent numerical gradings assist and boost the ego of high achievers but may significantly deter the focus of struggling students (Butler, 1988), and a continually glaring numerical or alphabetical label may, to some students, only scream: *I am a failure*. However, at the end of a module, after a range of assessments have been completed, a final numerical value, as Jensen and Barron (2014) claim, may work best as a summative 'checkpoint' for students, parents, and schools. These highly debated and considerately researched standpoints can be confusing, conflicting or frustrating for educators trying to implement effective policies. The key questions could be: is there purpose in delivering feedback that way, or in giving your student a grade at that particular point in your data capture? Does it/will it assist the learning process?

The contentions surrounding grade use, data validity, written marking, verbal feedback, group feedback, peer feedback, and no marking *whatsoever* all contribute to the imbroglios of implementing effective assessment. However, there are many educators who are working to remind us about exactly what can be achieved, and how best to move forward to ensure we continue to build assessment, marking and feedback policies that build the strongest bridge to our pupils' success. The key seems to be ensuring *purpose*.

How will this book help?

All of the debates above have to be considered as we build, plan and implement assessments so that we can ensure that we are working as effectively as possible to move our students forward. *The researchED Guide to Assessment* aims to assist teachers in building greater confidence and understanding of feedback and assessment methods so that data can be collected more accurately, and student progression can be assessed more clearly.

I am delighted that Dylan Wiliam has agreed to open this book with an astute and detailed summary of assessments and, in particular, their validity. There is no accident in beginning my introduction with a quote from Wiliam, who has led some of the most evocative conversations about assessment and learning in recent educational research across the world. In his opening chapter, he astutely explores the idea that assessment validity lies not in the assessment itself, but in the information we infer from the assessment. Furthermore, in an exciting turn away from normal educational discourse, Wiliam redefines what it means when we consider assessments to be 'formative' or 'summative', and reminds us about the functionality and purpose of assessment (and its data) when building academic schemes of work.[1]

Assessment validity and its counterpart data validity are universally prominent cogs in the machine that most successfully turns the wheel of effective assessment, marking and feedback. This is illuminated by the material and research provided by Rich Davies, leader of data and insight at Ark Schools, in his chapter of this book, 'Strength in Numbers'. Davies's chapter provides some clear direction as to how assessments can be managed more effectively within schools. Rich draws on his own research and data at Ark and provides some useful practical tools for a school in accordance with both internal and national data distribution.

Will Millard and Loic Menzies, both staff members of The Centre for Education and Youth, present their own innovative research on assessment with an international focus – in particular, the findings of Menzies's 'Making Waves',

---

1. What should you be asking to see if a test is valid or purposeful? Professor Robert Coe, now the director for research and evaluation at Evidence Based Education (EBE), asks educators: 'Would you let this test into your classroom?' His blog post consists of 47 succinct questions to enable middle leaders, senior leaders or heads of department to construct an effective contextual, data and marking system for each assessment. It can be accessed here: www.bit.ly/2Tg2sVA

a one-year research project which involved an in-depth study of teachers and aimed to find a better future for assessment. Will Millard's chapter compares curriculum and assessment between British Columbia and England, drawing some similarities and differences, evaluating what can be taken forward from this international perspective to improve areas of assessment, marking and feedback.

It is also a pleasure that Professor Dame Alison Peacock, CEO of the Chartered College of Teaching, has contributed a cohesive chapter on assessment of learning in primary school, allowing educators to refine the jumps between primary, secondary and senior education by encouraging learning without limits. In a similar way, deputy headteacher Ruth Powley writes about the pursuit of the powerful and the impact of using assessment to sustain this power amongst learners

Looking closer at subject-specific strategies, Kristopher Boulton's chapter explores the fundamental differences that exist between subjective subjects (such as humanities and English) and subjects with objective content (such as mathematics). Boulton compares the skills required to succeed in these areas and puts forward questions about whether assessment can, should, or does look the same in these subjects. Claire Hill and Freya Odell, both excellent English classroom practitioners, contribute their expertise to practical solutions in the classroom and encourage teachers to reflect on their own pedagogies to provide excellent assessment support and stability for pupils and make effective changes in English and whole-school marking policies.

Finally, Tom Sherrington closes the book with some key fundamentals of assessment, marking and feedback: the dos and don'ts. Sherrington's chapter is an effective and cohesive summary of grade boundaries, testing, data interpretation, assessment developing, and parental reporting – in short, the whole spectrum required to ensure that your assessment policy is, as he describes, *authentic*.

The debates around practices in assessment, marking and feedback are undoubtedly strong and varied, but the most important thing that we can do as educators is continue to try to find solutions that not only better the progress of our pupils but also assist the wellbeing and manageability of workload for our staff. Whilst these debates can be polarising, the value of researchers, teachers, policymakers and professionals in writing, exploring and publishing new ideas is vital. I hope these chapters encourage further discussion, spark new ideas, and provide more guidance about how these processes can occur within your school environments for the foreseeable academic years.

Bibliography

Butler, R. (1988) 'Enhancing and undermining intrinsic motivation: the effects of task-involving and ego-involving evaluation on interest and performance', *British Journal of Educational Psychology* 58 (1) pp. 1–14.

Christodoulou, D. (2018) 'Give me your answer do', *researchED* 2 (1) pp. 5–8.

Department for Education (2016) *Eliminating unnecessary workload around marking*. London: The Stationery Office. Retrieved from: www.bit.ly/3231ZJ5

Education Endowment Foundation (2018) 'Feedback', *Teaching and Learning Toolkit*. London: Education Endowment Foundation. Retrieved from: www.bit.ly/3cIKFxV

Elliot, V., Baird, J., Hopfenbeck, T. N., Ingram, J., Thompson, I., Usher, N., Zantout, M., Richardson, J. and Coleman, R. (2016) *A marked improvement? A review of the evidence on written marking*. London: Education Endowment Foundation. Retrieved from: www.bit.ly/2Y8lW15

Hattie, J. (1999) *Influences on student learning* [Inaugural professorial address, University of Auckland]. 2 August. Retrieved from: www.bit.ly/3fZS662

Hattie, J. and Timperley, H. (2007) 'The power of feedback', *Review of Educational Research* 77 (1) pp. 81–112.

Jensen, P. A. and Barron, J. N. (2014) 'Midterm and first-exam grades predict final grades in biology courses', *Journal of College Science Teaching* 44 (2) pp. 82–89.

Kime, S. (2018) *Reducing teacher workload: the 'Rebalancing Feedback' trial* [Research report]. Evidence Based Education.

Kime, S. and Lowe., J. (2018) *What happened when teachers stopped marking?* [Talk delivered at researchED National Conference 2018, London]. 8 September.

McMillan, J. H., Myran, S. and Workman, D. (2002) 'Elementary teachers' classroom assessment and grading practices', *The Journal of Educational Research* 95 (4) pp. 201–213.

O'Neill, M., Rasor, R. A. and Bartz, W. R. (1976) 'Immediate retention of objective test answers as a function of feedback complexity', *The Journal of Educational Research* 70 (2) pp. 72–75.

Ofsted (1998) *Subjects and standards: issues for school development arising from Ofsted inspection findings 1997/1998: key stages 3 and 4 and post-16.* London: The Stationery Office.

Ofsted (2018) *Annual report 2017/18: education, children's services and skills.* London: The Stationery Office.

Sadler, D. R. (1998) 'Formative assessment: revisiting the territory,' *Assessment in Education: Principles, Policy & Practice 5* (1), pp. 77–84.

Sweller, J. (1988) 'Cognitive load during problem solving: effects on learning', *Cognitive Science* 12 (2) pp. 257–258.

Wiliam, D. (2011) *Embedded formative assessment.* Bloomington, IN: Solution Tree Press.

Winne, P. H. and Butler, D. L. (1994) 'Student cognition in learning from teaching' in Husen, T. and Postlethwaite, T. (eds) *International encyclopedia of education.* 2nd edn. Oxford: Pergamon, pp. 5738–5745.

Author bio-sketch:

Sarah Donarski is an English teacher at Wellington College and is a curator of Wellington College's Festival of Education. She has spoken at researchED conferences around the UK and has been cited in the IB Review and other John Catt and Crown House publications. Sarah regularly blogs at perspected.wordpress.com. Her main area of research, feedback, has been her key focus for her own book, *Why Don't They Listen?*, published soon by Routledge.

HOW TO THINK ABOUT ASSESSMENT[2]

DYLAN WILIAM

Introduction

In most areas of education, there are few – if any – undisputed facts. Some believe that whole language, or 'balanced literacy', is the way to teach reading in the early years, while others argue for the importance of a foundation in structured synthetic phonics. Some argue for ability grouping, particularly for older learners, and in subjects like mathematics, while others point out the advantages of mixed-ability teaching. The important point here is that in such debates, the evidence is rarely as clear as we would like, and different people can, looking at the same evidence, reasonably come to different conclusions.

Educational assessment is different. While there are areas where reasonable people can disagree, there are also many areas where you can be not just out of the mainstream, but factually, demonstrably incorrect.

The aim of this chapter is to provide the reader with an understanding of some of the most important ideas in assessment – such as reliability, validity and so on – but also to show how the right ways of thinking about these ideas can lead to much more productive discussions about how to assess. The chapter also aims to help the reader understand that there is no such thing as a perfect assessment system. Every assessment system involves trade-offs, and what matters is whether the trade-offs made are more or less appropriate in particular situations. In this way, assessment can support learning as well as measuring it.

Assessments are procedures for drawing inferences

The word 'assessment' comes from the Latin *assidere* (originally, 'to sit with'). But then the word 'matinee' comes from the Latin *matutinus* ('early in the morning', after Matuta, the goddess of the dawn), so the origin of a word often bears no relationship to its current usage. Language evolves.

---

2.   With apologies to Jordan Ellenberg, author of *How Not to Be Wrong: The Power of Mathematical Thinking.*

More problematically, particularly in education, we have what Truman Kelley called the 'jingle-jangle' fallacies (Kelley, 1927). The jingle fallacy (originally proposed by Herbert A. Aikins) is to assume that things with the same label are in fact the same. The jangle fallacy is the opposite: assuming that things with different labels are in fact different.

Some people use the words 'assessment' and 'evaluation' interchangeably, while others give the two terms different meanings. To make things even worse, there is not even any consistency, amongst those who distinguish between assessment and evaluation, what the difference is. For example, in higher education, some use 'assessment' to mean the process of collecting and documenting evidence for the purpose of improving learning, while 'evaluation' is used for the process of assigning grades or scores to students' performance. In compulsory education, particularly in the US, it is more common to apply the term 'assessment' to individuals, and 'evaluation' to institutions, or artifacts such as curriculum. The important point here is that there is no consensus on the meanings of the terms 'assessment' and 'evaluation', so when we use these terms, it is useful to be clear about what we mean.

In this chapter, I am going to follow Lee J. Cronbach (1971) in defining 'assessment' as a procedure for drawing inferences. We give students things to do – such as tasks, activities, tests and so on – and we collect evidence from the students, from which we draw conclusions. The conclusions may be about status, such as 'this child knows 50% of his number facts' or 'this pupil is likely to be successful in training to be a doctor', or it could be about next steps in teaching, such as 'this child is having particular difficulty with the seven times table' or 'this student seems to be having particular difficulty with electron pair repulsion theory in their mock A level Chemistry exam'.

Defining an assessment as a procedure for drawing inferences also clarifies that it makes no sense to define the terms 'formative' and 'summative' as kinds of assessment, because the same assessment can be used summatively or formatively. In the example above, a test of number facts gave us evidence for both a summative conclusion (this child knows 50% of his number facts) and a formative one (this child would likely benefit from work on the seven times table). There is no such thing as *a* formative assessment or *a* summative assessment. There are, instead, formative and summative uses of assessment information. Now to be sure, some assessments may be better for summative functions, and some may be better for formative functions; but it is the inferences, and not the assessments themselves, nor even the evidence generated by those assessments, that are formative or summative.

Validity is a property of inferences, not of assessments

The idea that assessments are procedures for drawing inferences also helps clarify the idea of the validity of an assessment. Traditionally, 'validity' has been defined as the extent to which an assessment assesses what it purports to assess. However, there are two problems with this definition. The first is that assessments do not purport anything. The purporting (if there is such a word) is done by humans, and assessments are often used in ways that were never intended, or even envisaged, by the assessment developers. For example, GCSEs were originally intended to provide information about the extent to which a student had learned the contents of the syllabuses for their chosen subjects, ostensibly with a view to providing information about that student's potential for further study. However, GCSE grades are now used to inform judgements about the quality of education provided by the school that the student attends – a function they were never designed to fulfil (and do not do particularly well). A student's average GCSE grade may provide some information about the extent of that student's achievement on her GCSE courses, but it provides very little information about the quality of education received by that student, since the most important factors in a student's GCSE grades are nothing to do with the school, but rather the personal characteristics – and the social background – of the student (Wiliam, 2012).

The second problem with defining validity as a property of a test or other form of assessment is that an assessment can be valid in some circumstances but not others. If we had an arithmetic test with a high reading demand, what can we conclude from a student's score on the test? If the student is a fluent reader, then, provided the test samples all aspects of arithmetic, we can reasonably conclude that high scores indicate good arithmetic ability and low scores indicate weak arithmetic ability.[3] But if some of the students who take the test are weak readers, we do not know what a low score means. It might be that the student was unable to do the arithmetic, but it might mean that the student was able to do the arithmetic, but was unable to read the questions well enough to know what she was being asked to do. If we believe that validity is a property of a test, we would be in the curious situation of saying that the same test would be valid for some students but not others.

This is why there is now widespread agreement amongst assessment researchers that validity is not a property of assessments but of *inferences*. For a given

---

3.   The word 'ability' is used here in its most literal sense, which is how able a student is to do something, and does not imply that ability is in any sense fixed. If a student learns more, then ability increases.

assessment, some conclusions will be valid, but others will not. Whether a particular assessment can support valid inferences will depend on the students to whom it is given, but it will also depend on the circumstances under which the assessment is administered.

To see why the way an assessment is administered has an impact on what kinds of inferences are supported by the results yielded by the assessment, consider a spelling test in which students are asked to spell 20 words drawn at random from a word bank of 1000 words. If a student does not know which words have been chosen, then if a student spells 10 of the 20 words correctly, then it is reasonable to assume that the student knows how to spell approximately half of the 1000 words in the word bank. But if the student knows which 20 words will be on the test, then all we know is that the student knows how to spell the 10 words they spelled correctly in the test.

This example illustrates a very important principle in assessment. When we give students an assessment, we are hardly ever interested in how well a student did on that test. We are interested in how the results on the test allow us to draw conclusions about things that were *not* on the test. The more predictable an assessment is, the less information the test provides about the things that were not tested. This does not mean that tests should not be predictable – there are times when this is entirely appropriate – but it is important to realize that a predictable test tells us only about the things that were tested. The results a student gets on a test on adding three-digit numbers in which all the sums are in vertical format:

$$
\begin{array}{r}
5 \ \ 6 \ \ 4 \\
+ \ \ 3 \ \ 6 \ \ 7 \\
\hline
\\
\hline
\end{array}
$$

will not tell us whether a student can do the same calculation in horizontal format:

$$564 + 367 =$$

This is why validity cannot be a property of a test. A test is valid for some conclusions, but not others. This was nicely summed up by Cronbach (1971): 'One validates, not a test, but an *interpretation of data arising from a specified procedure.*' (p. 447, emphasis in original)

So, when someone asks, 'Is this test valid?' in my view the best response is, 'Tell me what you propose to conclude about a student when you see their test score, and I'll tell you whether that conclusion is justified.'

The focus on inferences, rather than assessments, also helps clarify the issue of bias in assessment. Regarding bias as a property of assessments runs into the same problems as regarding validity as a property of tests. After all, a test tests what a test tests. The bias comes when we conclude that a particular assessment outcome has a particular meaning. Bias, like validity, is a property of inferences, not of assessments.

There are two main threats to validity

There are two main reasons why the results from assessments may not support the conclusions we want to make. The first is that the assessment does not assess the sorts of things which we want to make inferences about – intuitively, the assessment is 'too small'. The second is that the assessment assesses things which are not relevant to the things which we want to make inferences about – the assessment is, in some sense, 'too big'.

Construct underrepresentation

The technical term for the first reason (when the assessment is too small) is 'construct underrepresentation'. The idea here is that we have a construct of interest – say science achievement – and the assessment does not cover all the things that we would need to know about a student to draw conclusions about the student's achievement on this construct.

Of course, whether this is an issue depends on how we define our construct of interest, but if we define science achievement so as to include practical skills, then our assessment must include practical assessments or else we cannot be sure that a student's performance on a written assessment is a good guide to their practical skills.

In response to this, people often counter by saying that the scores that students get on practical assessments correlate highly with their scores on written tests, so it is really a waste of money to include practical assessments; we can use the scores on the written assessment as a proxy for the scores on the practical assessment. While this may be true as long as teachers are including practical work in their curriculum, failing to assess all important parts of a subject makes it possible to increase a student's score on a test by ignoring the untested parts of the curriculum. When schools are under pressure to increase test scores, narrowing the curriculum to focus only on the things that are tested makes it easier to increase students' achievement on the things that are measured. This is a bit like putting ice cubes in the mouth of a patient with a fever. When you measure the patient's temperature with a thermometer in the mouth, you get a lower reading on the thermometer, but you haven't addressed the underlying issue, which is the fever. You have changed the indicator, but not the indicated.

Now it is important to realize that if a test or other form of assessment assesses all the important aspects of a subject but is used in a high-stakes setting, and teachers teach to the test, then that does not jeopardize the validity of the assessment. The assessment assesses everything it should. But if the assessment underrepresents the subject, such as a test of English language that does not assess speaking and listening, and in a high-stakes setting, teachers reduce the amount of time they spend on the untested aspects, then the validity of the assessment is in question, because it was the deficiencies in the assessment (the construct underrepresentation) that caused the adverse social consequences.

Construct-irrelevant variance

The technical term for the second issue is 'construct-irrelevant variance', which seems like the worst kind of psychological jargon, but it is worth taking time to understand this idea because it can help us think about assessment problems in more powerful and productive ways.

Recall the arithmetic test with a high reading demand discussed earlier. Ideally, with an arithmetic test, we would want differences in scores on the test to be associated with differences in arithmetic ability, and only differences in arithmetic ability. If all students taking the test are fluent readers, and the test is a good test of arithmetic, then variations in the scores achieved will be due to differences in arithmetic ability. But if some of the students are weak readers and the reading demand of the test is high, some of the variation in the scores on the test will be caused by differences in arithmetic ability and some by differences in reading ability. Variation in scores caused by variation in arithmetic ability is construct-relevant – after all, this is what we are trying to assess. But variation in scores caused by variation in reading skill is construct-irrelevant – differences in reading ability should not affect a student's score on an arithmetic test. And because statisticians tend to measure variation in scores by calculating the variance of a set of scores,[4] when scores are influenced

---

4.   To find the variance of a set of scores, we find the mean of all the scores and subtract each score from the mean. It makes no sense to average the resulting numbers because the mean will be zero, so first, we square each of these differences from the mean (thus getting rid of all minus signs) and find the average of the resulting numbers. This is the variance, and is a measure of how spread out the scores are.

by things that should not be influencing the scores, the scores are said to suffer from construct-irrelevant variance.

From the foregoing, it should be clear that construct-irrelevant variance is a property of a set of scores, not of the assessment itself. If we gave our arithmetic test to fluent readers, the variation in the scores would be construct-relevant (because the reading proficiency of the students taking the test would not be an issue). However, if some students taking the test are poor readers, then some of the variation in scores will be caused by differences in reading ability, so there would be a degree of construct-irrelevant variance in the scores. The variation in scores on a particular test might be construct-relevant for one group of students, but include some construct-irrelevant variation with another group of students.

The importance of construct definition

To see how these two threats to validity – construct underrepresentation and construct-irrelevant variance – can help clarify our thinking, it is useful to consider how we might assess a student's knowledge of history, and in particular, whether we can assess our students' knowledge of history just by using multiple-choice questions.

Some people say yes, and some people say no, and this debate appears to be a debate about the suitability of different methods of assessment; but in reality, people on different sides of this argument have different beliefs about what it means to be good at history – i.e., the construct of history.

For those who think history is all about facts and dates, multiple-choice questions are pretty nifty because you can assess a lot of facts and dates in a reasonably short period of time. Moreover, the 'facts-and-dates' brigade regard essay questions as inappropriate because while some of the variation in scores on such questions will be due to differences in historical knowledge, some of it will be due to differences in writing ability, and even handwriting speed. In other words, the 'facts-and-dates' brigade will regard scores on history assessments that involve essay writing as embodying some construct-irrelevant variance (those better at writing do better).

On the other hand, those who think that being good at history is more than just knowing facts and dates and also includes things like being able construct historical arguments will regard assessments made up entirely of multiple-choice questions as underrepresenting the construct of history. Students who are better at constructing historical arguments will do no better than those who are not if they do equally well on facts and dates.

The important point here is that the debate about how to assess history appears to be a debate about assessment methods, but in reality it goes much deeper. The debate does come to surface when we are talking about how to assess history, but in reality it is an argument about what it means to be good at history – it is an argument about how the construct of historical knowledge should be defined.

This matters, because if the construct has been defined properly, different people should agree about whether a particular set of assessments adequately samples the domain of interest. In other words, with good construct definition, assessment design is a largely technical matter. However, if the construct is not well-defined, then assessment design becomes a value-laden process. In particular, the values of the people designing the assessment play a part in the design of the assessment.

Now that we have tools for thinking about validity, it might seem obvious that we should turn our attention to the other desirable quality of assessments: reliability. However, we do not need to do so because we already have the tools we need, because reliability is actually part of validity.

(Un)reliability is an aspect of construct-irrelevant variance

As mentioned earlier, in the example of the arithmetic test with a high reading demand, when the test is given to both weak and strong readers, there is an element of construct-irrelevant variance in the scores. This construct-irrelevant variance is systemic in that it is likely to affect all poor readers in a similar way. However, some sources of construct-irrelevant variance are random. Students have good days and bad days, so the performance in a test on a particular occasion might not be typical of what that student would achieve on other occasions. One marker might give a student the benefit of the doubt on a particular question while another would not. The particular questions included in a test might suit some students better than others.

Traditionally, factors such as these have been regarded as issues of reliability, and people have talked about the need for assessments to be 'valid and reliable', implying that validity and reliability were separate properties of assessments. However, such a perspective makes little sense because if the results of an assessment are unreliable, then they cannot possibly support valid inferences. If the score a student gets tomorrow is very different from the score they got today, then any conclusions that you draw about that student's capabilities on the basis of today's test score are unlikely to be valid. Reliability is a pre-requisite for validity.

However, there seems to be a paradox here, because reliability is often seen to be in tension with validity, with attempts to increase reliability having a negative influence on validity. How can reliability be in tension with validity while at the same time be a pre-requisite for it?

The two threats to validity discussed above – construct underrepresentation and construct-irrelevant variance – provide a resolution of this paradox. Increasing reliability – for example by standardizing assessments, by giving markers strict marking guidelines, and focusing only on aspects of a subject that are easy to assess – may well reduce construct-irrelevant variance, but only at the expense of reducing the representation of the construct (or, in other words, *increasing* the amount of construct underrepresentation). Put simply, we are prioritizing the reduction of some threats to validity at the expense of others. For a given amount of assessment time, we can cast our net widely and get some not particularly reliable information about a large number of aspects of a subject, or we can focus our attention on much more limited aspects of a subject and get much more reliable information. And of course, there is no right answer here. Sometimes we need a floodlight to get a perspective on a wide area, and sometimes we need a spotlight, getting clear information about a small area. What matters is whether the trade-off between reliability and other aspects of validity is more or less appropriate for the particular situation.

This last point is particularly important because it is often assumed that more reliability is better, but unless we narrow the assessment (and therefore increase construct underrepresentation) the only way to make an assessment more reliable is to make it longer. Moreover, the increases in testing time needed to make assessments more reliable are substantial. For example, to reduce the number of students getting the wrong grade in a GCSE subject from 40% to 25% would require increasing the length of the exams in that subject fourfold.[5]

Because appreciable increases in the reliability of our assessments require so much extra assessment time – time that would be better spent on teaching our students – we need to understand how reliable our assessments are, so that

---

5.   The estimate is based on applying the Spearman-Brown prophecy formula to the data in the table on page 19 of Wiliam (2001).

we can make informed judgements about how much weight to place on the information they provide.

Reliability isn't everything, but it is important

The starting point for estimating the reliability of an assessment is to assume that a student has a true score on that assessment. When people hear the term 'true score', they assume that this means assuming that ability is fixed, but this is not the case. The true score is simply the long run average that a student would score over many administrations of a test, assuming that no learning takes place.

For example, returning to the 20-word spelling test discussed earlier, if the student actually knows how to spell 600 of the 1000 words in the word bank, her true score is 60%. If she learns how to spell another 100 words her true score will be 70%. If she forgets how to spell 100 of these words, her true score will be 50%. We could of course find a student's true score by testing her on all 1000 words in the bank, but we have better things to do with our (and her) time, so we take a random sample of all the things we might assess and use the student's score on the sample as an estimate of her score on the whole domain (in this case, the 1000 words in the word bank). The reliability of our test is simply an indication of how good the score on the test is as a guide to the student's proficiency on the whole word bank.

Suppose we ask a student to spell 20 of the 1000 words in the word bank, drawn at random, on five occasions over the course of the day, and her scores are 15, 17, 14, 15 and 14. On average, she scores 15 out of 20 (i.e., 75%) so our best guess is that she can spell 750 of the 1000 words.

If, on the other hand, the results had been 20, 12, 17, 10 and 16, her average score would still be 15 out of 20, so our best guess would still be that she knows 750 of the 1000 words, but now we would be much less confident that our samples were a good guide to the whole bank because the scores vary so much. An analogy might be helpful here. If you wanted to find out if your child had a fever, and had only an electronic thermometer available, then if you measured the child's temperature three times, and got 36.6°C, 37.4°C, and 37.0°C you would probably feel confident that your child did not have a fever (conventionally defined as a body temperature over 38.0°C). But if the readings you got were 35.0°C, 39.0°C, and 37.0°C, you might well be alarmed. In both cases, the average of the three readings is the same (37°C) but in the second case, the spread of the readings gives us little confidence in the readings.

To create a measure of how spread out our scores are, we subtract the average score from each score, so in the first example, we would get the following:

Actual score	15	17	14	15	14
Difference from average	0	+2	−1	0	−1

If we took the average of these five differences, we would get zero (that is, after all, the definition of the average), so we square each of the differences (to get rid of the minus signs), add up the totals, and then divide by the number of scores (in this case, five). We then take the square root of the result, which gives us the standard deviation of the errors, which in this case is 1.2.

Using the scores in the second example, we would get

Actual score	20	12	17	10	16
Difference from average	+5	−3	+2	−5	+1

The standard deviation of the errors here is 4.0, which tells us that the score that a student gets in this case would be a less accurate guide to the score a student might get on the whole test.

With a typical school test or other form of assessment, the errors will usually form a classic 'bell curve' or normal distribution, so we can use the properties of the normal distribution to see what these numbers mean. With a normal distribution, 68% of the data points fall within one standard deviation of the mean and 96% fall within two standard deviations of the mean. Therefore, if the standard deviation of the errors – often called the standard error of measurement or SEM – for all students was 1.2, then for approximately two-thirds of the students in a group, their score on any one assessment occasion will be within 1.2 points of their true score, and almost all (96%, or 24 out of 25) will get a score within 2.4 points of their true score.

If, however, the SEM is 4 points, then for two-thirds of the students, their actual score will be within 4 points of the true score, and for 96% of the students, their score will be within 8 points of the true score. However, for every class of 25, there will be one student who gets a score that is more than 8 points away from their true score. Unfortunately, we won't know which student this is, nor whether the score they got was too high or too low.

These of course are just examples. To find out what this looks like in practice, it is useful to see the errors of measurement that are typical with educational assessments. Most test publishers do report the standard errors of measurement of their assessments, but tend to give more prominence to a test's index of reliability. This ranges from 0 to 1, with a completely random assessment (i.e., one where a student's score is completely a matter of chance) having a reliability of 0 and a perfectly reliable assessment (where the student would get exactly the same score on every testing occasion) having a reliability of 1. To see how the SEM relates to the reliability, the table below shows the relationship for an assessment where the average score for all students is 50% and where almost all students score between 20% and 80% (i.e., a standard deviation of 15).[6]

For a typical test (average score 50, standard deviation 15), a student with a true score of 60 will, on a given occasion, score			
Reliability	SEM	Two-thirds of the time (68%)	Almost always (96%)
0.70	8.2	52 to 68	44 to 76
0.75	7.5	53 to 68	45 to 75
0.80	6.7	53 to 67	47 to 73
0.85	5.8	54 to 66	48 to 72
0.90	4.7	55 to 65	51 to 69
0.95	3.4	57 to 63	53 to 67

Teacher-produced tests typically have reliability indices in the range 0.70 to 0.80, while standardized tests have reliability from 0.90 to 0.95, and specialized psychological tests can have reliabilities over 0.95. The reliability of GCSE exams ranges from 0.70 to 0.95 with a mean value around 0.83 (Hayes and Pritchard, 2013)

Reliability data for the 2018 key stage 2 tests are shown in the table below (Thomson, 2019).

---

6. Formally, the relationship between the reliability index, r, and the standard error of measurement (SEM) is given by the formula $SEM = SD \times \sqrt{(1 - r)}$ where SD is the standard deviation of the scores of all the students taking the test. When r is zero, the SEM is equal to the SD of all the scores, because the test is providing no information about the student. Our uncertainty about a student's score is just as great after we are told the result (the SEM) as before (the whole group SD). When r is 1, then the SEM is zero, because there is no uncertainty about the student's result.

Test	Duration	Reliability	SEM (%)
Mathematics	110 minutes	0.96	5.3
Reading	60 minutes	0.90	5.9
Grammar, punctuation, spelling	60 minutes	0.95	4.5

In other words, in 2018, two-thirds (actually 68%) of students received a score within 5.9% of their true score in reading, within 5.3% in mathematics and within 4.5% in grammar, punctuation and spelling (GPS). However, in a class of 25 students, one student would have got a score at least 11% lower or higher than their true score in mathematics, at least 12% different from their true score in reading, and 9% off in GPS.

As noted above, this does not necessarily mean that we want more reliable tests. For example, to make the reading test as reliable as the maths test, we would need to increase the length of the test to 180 minutes, which might well bring additional problems such as student fatigue. Instead, the important message here is that the reliability of our tests may well be optimal. We do not necessarily need more reliable tests. What we do need is to be aware of the limitations of our assessments so that we do not place more weight on the result of an assessment than its reliability would warrant.

This is particularly important when looking at change scores – the change in a student's score over a period of time – because we are, in effect, subtracting one unreliable number from another unreliable number. Indeed, the unreliability of change scores has led some psychologists to conclude that we should not even try to measure change (Cronbach and Furby, 1970). The problem is that, in education, change is what we are mostly interested in. We have to measure change, because it is the most important thing in education, but we need to be cautious about the meanings of these change scores. For example, it is common to find that the standard error of measurement of, say, a standardized reading test is approximately the same as the progress that an average student makes in six months. In other words, we end up saying, 'Over the last six months, you have made six months' progress, give or take six months.'

Finally, it is worth looking to see how reliability and other aspects of validity interact when we use assessments to make decisions about how to group students. The table below shows how accurate our placement of students into four ability groups or 'sets' would be if we assign students to sets on the basis of a test with reliability of 0.9 and where the correlation of the score on the test with eventual mathematics achievement (what is sometimes called 'predictive validity') is 0.7 (both of these figures are about as good as we can expect).[7]

		...should be in...			
		set 1	set 2	set 3	set 4
Students actually placed in...	set 1	23	9	3	
	set 2	9	12	6	3
	set 3	3	6	7	4
	set 4		3	4	8

In other words, by looking at the numbers that are not in the leading diagonal of the table above, we can see that 50 of the students are in the 'wrong' set.

This is not to make an argument for or against ability group in schools – the research on this issue is nowhere near as clear-cut as some people claim, so judgment is required. It is to point out that even if our assessments are as good as the 'state of the art', they are far from perfect, and we need to be cautious in making decisions on the basis of test results, especially when these decisions have profound consequences for students.

Summary
The key conclusions of this chapter are:

There is no such thing as a valid test. Rather, validity is best thought of as a property of inferences based on test outcomes. An assessment will, depending how it is administered, support some inferences, but not others. Moreover, a test may support valid inferences for some students and not others. In a similar vein, there is no such thing as a formative assessment or a summative assessment, because formative and summative are properties of inferences, not of assessments.

There are two main threats to validity: construct underrepresentation and construct-irrelevant variance. Some assessments are, in a sense, too small. They do not provide us with information about things we need to know about to draw the conclusions we want to draw, so they underrepresent the construct of interest. Some assessments, on the other hand, are too large. They may assess

---

7.   I have also assumed that, as is typical, the higher-achieving sets are larger than those for lower-achieving students.

the thing we want to know about but students' results are also affected by things that are unrelated to the things we want to know about, so the scores students get vary for reasons that are irrelevant to the things we want to know about (hence construct-irrelevant variance).

Arguments about assessment methods are often (usually?) arguments about constructs. When people find it hard to agree on whether a particular assessment method is appropriate, it is often, and perhaps usually, because they disagree about what should be assessed.

(Un)reliability is the random component of construct-irrelevant variance. When student performance varies from occasion to occasion, when the same work is given different marks by different markers (or even the same marker on different occasions), when the particular selection of questions included in the assessment – when any of these influence a student's score, there is random variation in the scores that is irrelevant to the construct of interest.

Change scores are much less reliable than status scores. While we do need to know about change scores – after all, we want to know whether our students are getting better – we need to be especially cautious in interpreting change scores, because they are the result of subtracting one unreliable number from another.

More reliability is not necessarily better. Assessments have to be made much longer to have a significant impact on reliability, taking time away from teaching. Relatively low reliability may be optimal, provided we know how reliable an assessment is, and therefore, how much weight to place on it.

All assessment involves trade-offs. The most important concept in education is opportunity cost: time that you spend assessing your students is time that you (and they) do not have for other things. The key thing in assessment is being clear about why you are assessing, what conclusions you want to draw, and how well your evidence supports the conclusions you want to draw. Keep those three things in mind, and you won't go far wrong.

References

Cronbach, L. J. (1971) 'Test validation' in Thorndike, R. L. (ed.) *Educational measurement*. 2nd edn. Washington, DC: American Council on Education, pp. 443–507.

Cronbach, L. J. and Furby, L. (1970) 'How we should measure "change" – or should we?', *Psychological Bulletin* 74 (1) pp. 68–80.

Hayes, M. and Pritchard, J. (2013) *Estimation of internal reliability*. Coventry: Ofqual.

Kelley, T. L. (1927) *Interpretation of educational measurements*. Yonkers-on-Hudson, NY: World Book Company.

Thomson, D. (2019) 'How reliable are key stage 2 tests?', *FFT Education Datalab* [Blog], 3 April. Retrieved from www.bit.ly/2yLKdjZ

Wiliam, D. (2001) 'Reliability, validity, and all that jazz', *Education 3–13* 29 (3) pp. 17–21.

Wiliam, D. (2012) 'Are there "good" schools and "bad" schools?' in Adey, P. S. and Dillon, J. (eds) *Bad education: debunking myths in education*. Maidenhead: Open University Press, pp. 3–15.

Author bio-sketch:

Dylan Wiliam is emeritus professor of educational assessment at UCL. In a varied career, he has taught in inner-city schools, trained teachers, directed a large-scale testing program, and served a number of roles in university administration, including dean of a school of education. His research focuses on supporting teachers to develop their use of assessment in support of learning.

ASSESSMENT AND FEEDBACK: AN EFFICIENCY MODEL FOR ENGLISH

CLAIRE HILL

There is no more valuable resource in schools than time, and there is likely no aspect of teaching that takes disproportionately more time than it has impact than giving ineffective feedback. This ineffectiveness is not simply an issue of quality, but also of efficiency. Taking English teaching as an example, individual comments that are well constructed, actionable, and personalised may be effective in terms of quality, but if it's inefficient to give them in terms of time, workload, singularity of purpose, or transferability, then the approach isn't really effective at all.

Feedback limitations

In practice, giving high-quality feedback that addresses the issue of both workload and impact suffers from a number of limitations:

- It focuses on the task or question rather than helping the student improve in future tasks.
- Students don't understand it or it isn't actionable.
- It involves setting assessments for the purpose of data drops rather than learning.
- It involves setting assessments that make it difficult to identify with precision the specific areas students need to improve.
- It involves over-complicated approaches that shift the focus to what the teacher is doing rather than what the student is doing.

The complexity of designing tasks that allow the teacher to both effectively identify the student's needs and give feedback on how to address those needs clearly takes a lot of thought. Often, the default approach is for students to answer numerous GCSE-style questions or for the teacher to write detailed, individual comments on students' work. However, these are likely to be the least effective or efficient way to do either. What we need in schools is a number of approaches to assessment and feedback that are manageable and realistic in terms of time and workload and that work together to allow the teacher to assess what students know and can do, give feedback that identifies specific areas to improve and help students to do so.

The inefficiency of individual written feedback

Written feedback on student work has long been considered a proxy for good teaching, with more frequent and longer comments correlated with teacher effectiveness. However, there is now a plethora of research that indicates writing on a piece of work is often a highly ineffective way of giving feedback.

The possible reasons for this may be that:

- **Only the student whose work is written on is benefiting from that feedback** whilst others, who perhaps have not made the mistake on this particular piece of work but who may do so in a future piece of work, do not receive the benefit of this advice.
- **Long written comments that are descriptive** (such as 'well done, you have included several good examples but you need to include more detail') provide very little in terms of actionable advice and focus on the work itself rather than future learning – what Wiliam (in Hendrick and Macpherson, 2017) identifies as being feedback that improves the work and not the student.
- **Too much feedback on several areas with lots of specific direction can be overwhelming** as it requires the student to attempt to improve too much and can contribute to a sense of complacency as students know any mistakes they make will be addressed for them and therefore do not properly engage with the task itself or the feedback that comes after.

The opportunity cost involved in the significant time and workload of teachers giving this individual feedback means not only that it is less effective than other approaches but also that this time is then not spent on making refinements to lessons or curriculum that may arguably have more impact on students' progress.

Instead, a blend of simplified whole-group feedback combined with efficient baseline testing and a granular approach to assessment through multiple-choice quizzes can offer a more effective way to identify what we reteach and practise with our students, whilst also reducing workload for the teacher.

Addressing inefficiencies in whole-group feedback

Many schools have moved to a policy of whole-group feedback in which teachers look at students' work and give feedback by addressing common misconceptions, reteaching key components, and giving personalised tasks for students to complete. All of this can be achieved without the need for written comments on every piece of work. However, even this approach has begun to suffer from overcomplication and reduced efficiency.

Whole-group feedback has been delivered in a variety of ways. One particular type is often combined with individual codes where students are given their letter or number and are asked to make changes or complete tasks based on their individual code. Students still receive personalised feedback but workload is dramatically reduced as a class of students will often make similar or the same mistakes, meaning the teacher only needs to devise a small number of codes and tasks for students to respond to and only needs to write these once, rather than on every piece of work. This process seems to be infallible.

However, the implementation of this approach can fall foul of overcomplication for two key reasons:

- Feedback sheets involve filling in lots of different boxes so effectiveness is reduced.
- Lots of different sections result in overly complex and crowded documents which are cognitively overloading.

More effective is a simple table with four sections: one that highlights areas to praise and specific models of this from students' work; one addressing misconceptions including spelling and grammar; a third box that includes an exemplar piece of work; and a final box that links students' personalised codes to specific tasks. The students' personalised task should focus on one aspect of their work and be both precise and immediately actionable. By doing this, we explicitly shift the marking process from feedback to advice giving (Yoon et al., 2019), using an actionable approach to ensure students focus on applying advice to future learning rather than simply receiving feedback on work already done.

In addition to ensuring whole-group feedback is effective by focusing on giving precise and actionable feedback, there are a number of methods that can complement this approach to ensure marking and feedback addresses the specific needs of each student, whilst still ensuring workload is manageable.

Whole-group feedback – simplified template	
Praise	**Model/exemplar**
This section can be used to share specific examples of what students have done well and to discuss what makes these examples effective so that a similar approach can be used by others next time. This is much more effective than using vague praise such as 'lots of good analysis'. Using ideas and examples from students' work in your class is also an opportunity to celebrate their work and to show what is possible. This evidence of success from those in your class can offer motivation.	The model or exemplar is ideally written together in lesson or live modelled by the teacher; this section is therefore left blank so that students can be shown the process. Alternatively, a pre-written model can be used from exam materials, from students' work, or a teacher model to exemplify the final outcome. This should be relatively short so that the teacher can focus on specific elements that have been done well and that can be practised and emulated by students. If using a pre-written model, this should be deconstructed and annotated in the lesson. Having the model on the same sheet also means this is easy to find and return to later.
Misconceptions	**Next steps**
This could include common spelling errors or more substantive misconceptions such as those regarding plot, context or written expression. Having a separate section can more sharply focus our attention when giving feedback to help the teacher specifically look out for misconceptions and address them, which means these can be re-taught. This section may also influence decisions about how to teach this element the next time.	Next steps should be precise and actionable, giving students an opportunity to improve their work by practising an element they did less well but also allowing them to apply this to a new idea or piece of work. Students should not be given more than one or two clear next steps so that these can be deliberately practised and are not overwhelming. These next steps should be personalised based on their work so a student may just have '2' written on their work and know to complete task 2. However, having these next steps visible to all students means they can all benefit from this advice.

Whole-group feedback – example – *Macbeth* extract analysis	
Praise ✓ Analysis of the verb 'peep' when describing heaven ✓ Exploration of the antithesis of 'milk' and 'gall' ✓ The hypnotic rhythm of the speech and its incantation-like effect ✓ Echoes of speeches by Macbeth and/or the witches ✓ Significance and effect of the repetition of 'come' three times ✓ Allusion to *Hamlet* and its effect	**Model/exemplar** _____ _____ _____ _____ _____ _____ _____ _____
Misconceptions ✗ Remember, this play is Jacobean and not Elizabethan – this is important due to the royal propaganda in the play ✗ This soliloquy is just after Lady Macbeth is told 'the king comes here tonight' – it's important you remember where in the plot this is as her reaction to the news and our knowledge of the king influences how we feel towards Lady Macbeth ✗ Ensure expression is sophisticated, e.g. instead of 'witchy number' perhaps use 'a number associated with witchcraft' ✗ Which is the correct spelling: King Duncan will now be _____ to Lady Macbeth's schemes? a. vunerable b. vulnerable c. vulerable	**Next steps** 1. Edit your work so that all of your quotations are embedded, e.g. 'Lady Macbeth commands the "spirits" to "take [her] milk for gall".' Once you have done this, write sentences embedding the following quotations (you will need to remember who and what they refer to in your explanation): 'Stars, hide your fires' 'Look like the innocent flower' 2. Using the models and the ideas we've discussed to help you, choose another word or image to analyse and try to think of at least two to three connotations or interpretations. 3. Draw a mindmap of the contextual factors that may influence the interpretation of this scene. Link your ideas to specific moments/quotations from the soliloquy and explain their significance.

The value of establishing a baseline

Before we can start to give effective feedback, it is imperative to know the students we are teaching. Finding an efficient way to quickly gather useful information about our students when we first meet a new class means we can start to unpick where support may be required and make alterations to our curriculum or intervention plans accordingly.

These alterations need not be drastic and may simply inform seating plans or which key vocabulary needs to be pre-taught for a new topic. For example, a carefully constructed baseline assessment can be very useful for this early identification of needs.

> **Teaching idea:** a short exercise in which the teacher dictates a passage from a text for students to write, ideally with the passage chosen for both challenge and access, can give the teacher a whole host of information within the first lesson of taking a class.

The above task quickly provides (1) the teacher with information about the students' proficiency in spelling, handwriting, listening, processing, and (2) the attention to detail which will help quickly inform the teacher of areas that need to be addressed.

This exercise offers a snapshot of literacy levels that can be useful in establishing a baseline for areas that are less easy to identify through CATs or SATs results. In addition, repeating similar exercises over the course of the year can give some indication of progress and effort over time. Variations to this could include asking students to use more sophisticated synonyms at specific points during the passage or directing them towards sentence structures to employ, for example telling students that the next sentence is a complex sentence with an embedded subordinate clause and asking them to punctuate this accurately. The efficiency of such an assessment means that, without increasing workload, teachers have a very early indication of what the students in front of them know and can do and, within just a couple of lessons, can begin to address their needs.

Focusing feedback on individual components

Once a baseline is established, assessment is required to determine what students know and what they still need to know as they move through the curriculum. In order to take a more forensic approach to identifying what students have learnt, assessment and feedback should focus on individual components rather than moving straight to holistic, summative assessments.

In many schools, the focus of assessment is often skewed towards summative assessments that attempt to display progress – sometimes arbitrarily and sometimes falsely. This is often as a result of data drops that fit neatly into a school calendar or an attempt to demonstrate 'progress' and see grades or scores rising every half term. However, this approach to summative assessment – with each student writing full essays or completing full papers every few weeks in order to demonstrate progress – is unlikely to help that student to improve. There is not enough time between assessments for them to learn and practise the areas they need to work on; but also, when we assess holistically in this way, it is more difficult to home in on the precise areas that need to be reviewed, re-taught, and deliberately practised.

The study of English requires developing cumulative skills, which means that progress requires knowledge, both procedural and substantive, to accumulate over time. Assessment points that focus on extended writing should be spaced quite far apart to allow for this to accumulate and give time to learn and practise the many components required to write a formal essay. **Therefore, there need only be two or three summative assessments per year.**

Example assessment schedule – term 1

Assessment	MCQ	Quotation quiz	MCQ	Structuring sentences	Writing introductions	MCQ	Context quiz	Summative
Date	12/9	14/9	19/9	21/9	24/9	30/9	7/10	20/10

In the meantime, breaking down and practising the smaller individual components required for the final essay may prove more effective (and reduce time spent marking). Such components could measure a student's ability to structure sentences, embed quotations, write introductions, use appropriate contextual references, and so on. Moreover, explicitly teaching, practising and giving feedback on those individual elements allows the teacher and student to be far more precise about how to improve the work, and the student is much more likely to be successful in writing a formal essay.

More regular assessments of knowledge in English, particularly in the form of low-stakes multiple choice tests, can effectively assess how securely pupils have learnt the grammar, vocabulary, contextual information and concepts that will need to be synthesised in an extended piece of work. The benefit of this is twofold: it ensures that those elements can be assessed and fed back on even if they are not demonstrated in the final piece; and it allows the teacher to identify and respond to individual components and address specific misconceptions, such as misunderstanding of plot or contextual information, that may otherwise be missed when predominantly using extended tasks.

The efficiency of multiple-choice quizzes

Multiple-choice quizzes (MCQ) are increasingly being used in the classroom. This form of test is sometimes considered inappropriate for arts and humanities subjects and better left to the sciences. However, a well-structured MCQ can be extremely powerful, in terms of both identifying what students know and dealing with misconceptions.

Daisy Christodoulou (in Hendrick and Macpherson, 2017), by expanding on the work of Dylan Wiliam (in Hendrick and Macpherson, 2017), provides excellent advice on how to structure multiple-choice questions. Christodoulou suggests avoiding using answers that are obviously incorrect and instead designing questions with answers that are plausible but still unambiguously wrong. In addition, she recommends not telling students how many correct answers there are as this significantly reduces the likeliness of guesswork. However, for novice learners or those at the early stage of study, providing the number of possible answers to begin with can be used as a scaffold to help access the question and avoid cognitive overload. These guidelines help to increase the effectiveness of this form of testing; the examples below combine these ideas.

Examples in English:

Year 7
Which of the following sentences have an adverb underlined?
1. *Romeo and Juliet* is one of Shakespeare's best-known <u>plays</u>.
2. The language used in the play is <u>beautifully</u> lyrical.
3. The two young protagonists <u>quickly</u> fall in love.
4. Lord Capulet is adamant that his <u>lovely</u> daughter will marry the suitor he has chosen for her.
5. The prologue forewarns the audience that the play will end <u>tragically</u>.

Year 10
Which of the following characters are killed at the hands of Macbeth?
1. Banquo
2. King Duncan
3. Lady Macbeth
4. Macduff
5. Macdonwald

1. The year 7 example helps to identify the common misconception that 'lovely' is an adverb (due to its '-ly' suffix) and at the same time requires the student to be able to identify adjectives by process of elimination. The question therefore asks more of the student than just the definition and identification of an adverb.
2. The year 10 *Macbeth* question allows for interesting discussions surrounding blame whilst offering an opportunity for retrieval practice of the plot. When thoughtfully designed, these questions lend themselves to further elaboration and can offer a springboard for analysis or evaluation which take students beyond retrieval and towards a more detailed understanding.

Although clearly a useful tool for testing substantive knowledge, MCQs can also be used to assess students' disciplinary and procedural knowledge, allowing the teacher to test students' understanding of not only the content but also how to apply it, before they attempt or re-attempt an extended piece of work. This approach means issues can be addressed before students move to the next stage and their errors and misconceptions can be more sharply identified rather than having to be untangled from an extended piece. In addition, the process of designing MCQs can be a particularly useful exercise for novice teachers as it draws attention to the possible misconceptions students may have and how to both plan for and address these.

To further increase the effectiveness of this form of assessment and to help students to better respond to feedback, research by Stock et al. (in press) suggests that the use of confidence scores can encourage a hypercorrection effect which will help students to learn from any mistakes they may have made.

When completing MCQs, students can be asked to add a confidence score of 1–5 for each question with 5 indicating that the student is absolutely confident of their answer and 1 being not confident at all.

Dickens wrote and published *Great Expectations* in 1860–61. What do we call the period in which Dickens was writing?

1.	The Elizabethan era
2.	The Victorian era
3.	The Jacobean era
4.	The 19th century
5.	The 18th century

How confident are you of your answer? 1 = not confident 5 = very confident	

By doing so, if students find that a question they gave a confidence score of 5 is incorrect, they are more likely to learn the correct answer to that question due to the hypercorrection effect. To enhance this further and more specifically address the misconceptions that resulted in the incorrect answers, students can be asked, when appropriate, to write next to their confidence score why they have chosen this answer. This approach allows the teacher to better understand and address where the misconceptions have arisen.

If choosing to forgo confidence scoring, delaying the feedback on this type of test has been suggested to improve learning – a phenomenon that is attributed to the spaced effect and students forgetting their incorrect answers, as well as the increased attention to feedback that occurs after a delay (Kulhavy and

Anderson, 1972). However, combining the approach of confidence scoring and delayed feedback does not increase effectiveness.

Stock et al. (in press) suggest that delayed feedback undermines the use of confidence scores as these are not typically stored in long-term memory, and therefore delayed feedback will limit the effectiveness of hypercorrection. Regardless of whether feedback is immediate or delayed, it is important that students are given time to go through the answers to these questions and rectify their mistakes and misconceptions to ensure that the incorrect answers they have given do not become embedded in long-term memory. Clearly then, the method of feedback (and when it is given) needs to be considered when we design and administer the assessment.

Conclusion

For too long, a supposed proxy for good teaching has been how much a teacher writes on a piece of work, but this is often a poor indicator. We do not need to sacrifice ourselves at the altar of individual written feedback; we can find ways to make our feedback just as effective (if not more so) by employing a complement of approaches that identify where and how our students can improve their work whilst also reducing workload. Therefore, our time should be spent using students' work to help us refine our curriculum, plan what to re-teach, address misconceptions, and offer precise, specific feedback on granular components to ensure that we improve the student and not just the task.

Key takeaways

- When considering feedback and assessment policy, we need to keep a sharp focus on the efficiency of the methods we choose.
- Individual written comments suffer from a number of limitations and are often a poor proxy for effective feedback.
- Whole-group feedback has the dual benefit of focusing attention on what needs to be retaught and practised whilst reducing workload.
- Base lines tests through dictation tasks can help the teacher quickly gather a whole host of information to help support their students and can also be used to gauge progress over time.
- Deliberately practising individual components can help ensure feedback is precise and specific before moving to extended pieces of writing.
- Multiple-choice quizzes can be used to effectively identify misconceptions and check understanding.

References

Hendrick. C, and Macpherson, R. (2017) *What does this look like in the classroom? Bridging the gap between research and practice.* Woodbridge: John Catt Educational.

Kulhavy, R. W. and Anderson, R. C. (1972) 'Delay-retention effect with multiple-choice tests', *Journal of Educational Psychology* 63 (5) pp. 505–512.

Stock, W. A., Kulhavy, R. W., Pridemore, D. R. and Webb, J. M. (in press) 'Retrieving responses and confidence estimates for multiple-choice questions', *British Journal of Psychology.*

Yoon. J, Blunden. H, Kristal. A. and Whillans, A. (2019) *Framing feedback giving as advice giving yields more critical and actionable input.* HBS Working Paper 20-021. Cambridge, MA: Harvard Business School.

Author bio-sketch:

Claire Hill is trust improvement lead for Turner Schools and is networks officer for Litdrive UK. Claire has presented at a number of education conferences, written articles for the Royal Society of Chemistry and *Impact* magazine and is co-organiser of researchED Kent. Claire is also co-author of *Symbiosis: The Curriculum and The Classroom.*

SWIMMING AGAINST THE TIDE: ASSESSMENT OF LEARNING IN ONE PRIMARY SCHOOL

ALISON PEACOCK

Introduction

This chapter is a personal account of my endeavour to engage in meaningful assessment as a primary and early years teacher. I briefly document key influences on my thinking and then describe the culture and research engagement at the school where I was headteacher – a primary school that ultimately led the way in abandoning national curriculum levels across England.

The sorry tail of differentiation

The 'sorry tail' is taken from the title of a ground-breaking article by Susan Hart in which she challenged the notion that the accepted classroom practice of 'differentiation' was a helpful concept. Her view was that so-called 'ability' is a construct that seeks to separate rather than connect learners, with the unintended consequence of labelling leading to poverty of opportunity for some with an unfair benefit to others. A large gap (tail) was becoming evident, and in her opinion the practice of differentiation was making this worse:

> One major consequence [of viewing intelligence as fixed] is that it creates a disposition to accept the inevitability of limited achievement on the part of a significant proportion of the school population. It makes us fundamentally pessimistic about children's capabilities as learners and about our own power to intervene effectively. (Hart, 1998)

At the time, this idea was a radical one. To teach without differentiating was to ignore the prevailing view of the teacher's role. Hart's work led to the subsequent research study *Learning without Limits* (Hart et al., 2004). I was fortunate to be one of the nine teachers whose classroom formed part of this research. The study set out to research classrooms in primary and secondary schools where pupils were not underestimated according to notions of 'ability'. The award-winning book, published in 2004, set out to challenge limiting views of 'fixed ability' towards notions of 'transformability' through pedagogical practices that sought to build learning capacity. This work recognised the unconscious bias that children from marginalised communities often encountered and sought to highlight an alternative approach of high expectations for all.

An alternative school improvement model

When I was interviewed for headship, I shared my vision for the school as a 'listening school' and I told the governing body that under my leadership the school would become known as a 'centre of excellence'. At the time, the school had been categorised as 'requiring special measures' by Ofsted, and my optimistic vision must have appeared starkly at odds with the day-to-day reality of constant monitoring and termly HMI inspections where no progress had been noted in three years.

From those earliest days of headship of a primary school, my core ambition was to provide an example of a school where children and adults were valued and where no-one would be labelled or unintentionally held back. I was rapidly joined by a team of education researchers from the University of Cambridge, who were keen to study the notion of 'learning without limits' as a whole-school mission. An unswerving belief began to permeate the school that energy and expertise should always be used to 'find a way through' for every child. This positivity enabled a culture of success and resisted a deficit view of learners and education.

In my view, the alternative approach that our leadership team took to school improvement is important to note. Instead of blaming the incumbent teachers for the school's poor performance, we began to work as a team to encourage deep collegiate professional learning. Incessant 'monitoring' was replaced with coaching and mentoring. Professional learning and high ambition engaged the teachers, the wider team and the children in turn. The school was in the top one hundred most improved schools the following year and within three years was judged by Ofsted to be 'outstanding' in all categories. None of this had been achieved through the accepted school improvement methodology of the time but through leadership of learning and the adoption of a rich, culturally diverse curriculum, expertly taught.

The school became known nationally for high standards, inclusive innovation and creativity (2003–2016). The school was taken off special measures in 2003, and subsequently three full inspections by Ofsted found it to be 'outstanding' in every category (2006, 2009, 2013). A maths subject survey inspection took place in 2016 due to the school's exceptional results.

The children and teachers knew the importance of being listened to and of listening to each other. Dialogue that supports learning for every child was at the heart of this school with recognition given that dialogue builds cognition. Children were actively encouraged to describe their thoughts and actions and to enact their ideas within a rigorous and ambitious whole-school framework established by the entire teaching team. In mathematics, for example, the act of thinking aloud whilst explaining their method often embedded their understanding. Research experts such as Professor Robin Alexander visited the school to lead work on dialogic teaching (2004).

Twice yearly, at a learning review meeting, the older children formally presented a summary of their learning to their parents, teacher and to me as their headteacher. Throughout the year, they noted their successes and challenges as a means of beginning a written dialogue with their teacher on their end-of-year reports. The format of the report embodied the school ethos. The children self-assessed their learning experiences and summarised these using an electronic report format. Their teacher then accessed their report and continued the conversation, providing feedback and observations on their self-review. I reviewed the entire document before adding a comment of my own at the end. Families were keen to read their child's report, because it was a highly individualised document that offered an authentic overview of their child's achievements and next challenges. Comments from the family were added and these were returned to school for review. This process appears simple but it embodies the culture and ethos of a primary school where no-one's future success was pre-determined or narrowed. Grades were not used.

Freedom to think

Leadership that builds a culture of openness and trust enables professional learning to flourish. Creativity, quirkiness and eccentricity pervaded our school. There was a double-decker bus on the playground that served as a library, art therapy room and nurture space. A full-sized thatched Celtic roundhouse provided a magical storytelling space within grounds that were developed by children and the local community to grow fruit and vegetables. An outdoor music garden provided space for up to a hundred children and adults to perform together, drumming on saucepans, car bonnets and a kitchen sink. The overall sense was that this school provided a space to think differently and to celebrate a love of learning and life. Many teachers and support staff were supported to engage in postgraduate and degree-level study. This culture of career-long learning and innovation echoed our approach to assessment throughout the school. We wanted to think differently and to optimise our time in doing what was most likely to be transformative, rather than following others in pursuit of compliance.

In 2012, the work of the research team was published in *Creating Learning without Limits* (Swann et al., 2012). My role as insider-researcher meant that over many years I had the privilege of meeting regularly with the team to explain my thinking as a leader and to describe and record the impact of decisions taken. This work was undertaken alongside ongoing analysis of research interviews with colleagues, children and parents. This support and recognition of core purposes meant that the drive for school improvement increasingly focused on the response of the academic research team and less and less on the demands of the current inspection framework. Consequently, our school improvement agenda transcended that of the national inspection focus.

The school achieved a great deal of attention when in 2014 the UK government decided to remove the English national assessment system that had been based on levels of attainment. The vast majority of schools had used national curriculum levels as a means to provide a shorthand judgement of individual children's progress and, by association, the performance of their teachers. In our school, we used assessment to inform our teaching and to provide formative and summative feedback to children. Under my leadership, apart from participation in national end-of-key-stage testing, we resisted thinking about children's capacity to learn in terms of levels. Teachers were increasingly skilled at judging how much progress had been achieved and we used this to complete a very simple annual tracking form. Instead of talking with children, parents or colleagues about grades or levels, we discussed progress achieved to date and planned forward in ways that built upon this knowledge. Emphasis was placed on building opportunities for dialogue that provided detailed formative feedback to support future learning. This approach fundamentally ensured that the door was kept open for every child and meant that children's capacity to surprise us with new learning was always there. Teachers were awarded pay rises for their overall achievements with their class across the year without recourse to data sheets as 'proof'. This built a culture of collective ambition and a shared endeavour to achieve mutual success. Competitiveness was capitalised as a positive force for 'personal best' and self-improvement. The struggle was to constantly seek ways of gaining insight into what had been learnt during lessons in order to plan for the next steps that offered sufficient challenge. 'What has been learnt today that I can revisit and build upon tomorrow?' The importance of consolidation through deliberate practice was also recognised.

Whole-class feedback

Using a visualiser as a means to share examples of children's work meant that teachers were able to explain misconceptions or highlight common errors in a manner that provided helpful feedback. Children were not set targets but kept a list at the back of their books of specific areas they knew they needed to improve.

The year 5 and 6 teaching teams introduced a checking system for marking during independent work in the lesson to enable the children to see that they were completing maths tasks correctly. The children checked the answers every three or four questions (indicated by a star on the question sheet) at a 'marking station'. They were able to look at answers that showed the required working out and were asked to show that they understood any differences in their answers compared to the given answers. If they did not understand why their answer was incorrect, they were encouraged to talk to an adult.

Children across the school were encouraged to become independent and confident writers. During a unit of work, they drafted their work in their English books and were given brief 'topline' guidance by the class teacher during this process. This might be through verbal feedback or having spelling errors underlined. They were actively encouraged to continuously read through, edit and re-draft their work until they were satisfied with the final version. Editing showed adults the developmental process of the work and the progression of understanding. The final version was written out using best presentation skills. Only at this point would the teacher give detailed written feedback. This was finely tuned to the developmental needs of the individual child and consisted of a combination of praise and detailed advice about the improvement of technical skills. From this written feedback, the children identified next steps to apply across all areas of their written work. This form of written feedback was only given two or three times per term. These teachers subsequently became involved with work at the DfE to reduce teacher workload and to develop maths mastery.

Parental feedback

As an alternative to the traditional parents' evening model, where teacher and parents face each other across a table for ten minutes, learning review meetings were developed. We offered all parents of children in years 5 and 6 a learning review appointment. These meetings were 15 minutes long and were held in the headteacher's office. Each child prepared a brief presentation about their successes and challenges, using several PowerPoint slides. The child sat at my desk and gave a brief presentation of successes and challenges across the full curriculum. This was followed by a discussion directly involving the child about how we could collectively support their learning. The teacher brought their assessment notes and the books were put out on the coffee table so that we could all see examples of the work that was being completed.

The advantages of this process are many. As headteacher, I met with each year 5 and year 6 child with their teacher and family twice yearly and gained powerful insight into the progress being made. However, as a participant in these meetings over time, I was also visibly committing myself to ensuring that anything promised during the meeting would be delivered. There was no hiding place. This offered rigorous collective accountability to the child and the family.

The format of meetings meant that typically there would be meetings organised throughout a full day with a separate evening for additional appointments. This meant in a one-form entry school I dedicated two full days and two evenings in the autumn and spring terms to meet with 60 children and their parents. I had a file that built over time where I recorded the key challenges each child identified about their learning and the actions that we all agreed in the meeting that we would take to help. These could be very simple things, but impact was achieved when we followed these through consistently both at home and at school.

It was rewarding to see the children accelerate their progress during the final two years of primary school. They arrived for the learning review meeting with a mixture of excitement and trepidation. Children prepared several slides, often including whizzy graphics and features incorporating images such as photographs from their class blog. The meeting began with the child welcoming everyone to their learning review followed by a brief presentation. Once the presentation had been made, the teacher picked up on challenges and successes identified and provided their own feedback directly to the child about progress and areas for further development. This feedback was never about grades or future grades but was specific to the areas of learning that have been covered in class.

Parents were almost always delighted to witness their child's confident presentation, to hear the dialogue between teacher and learner and to see examples of their child's work. They were encouraged to support the child in addressing the next steps for their learning, which could be as diverse as practising spellings, encouraging more reading or rehearsing for a forthcoming play or concert. This was a rigorous review process that encouraged the highest expectations of every individual.

'Finding a way through' for every child

Thinking about classes I have taught and individual children that I recall, it is those who find it hard to submerge themselves totally into a class persona that are also the ones who add something different. They often bring a spark, force us to engage with them uniquely, disrupt our plans.

Of course, if we want to place efficiency first, these children are inconvenient. They may not learn at the same pace as others – either far too quickly or slowly; they may feel compelled to tell you and anyone else who will listen about something that is burning them up so that they cannot stay quiet. Ironically, some children, tussling with intellectual dilemmas and with an intense desire to acquire knowledge, may feel out of place in school and indeed may underperform in tests. One of our year 6 students, Arzu, loved problem solving and consequently decided to tackle questions from the back of the exam paper first when she sat an entry examination for secondary school. Boredom through gathering easy marks evidently was a worse prospect than tackling interesting time-consuming questions. She has recently graduated from Oxford.

I recall teaching John in year 5. He loved science and technology and would take almost anything to pieces to delight in its construction and to enjoy the puzzle of piecing it back together. Socially, he was awkward. He chewed his nails, refused to sit still, was irrepressibly excitable and loathed any form of written work. His exercise book was full of crossing out and re-working. The presentation in his books was appalling. He was an avid reader and frequently became so absorbed that he had to be reminded to put his book to one side and participate in lessons. I have recently heard that John, having gained a PhD from the University of Cambridge, is contributing to important scientific advances. It occurs to me that other polite members of my class who sat quietly and produced beautiful writing are unlikely to be contributing to scientific knowledge in a similar manner. We need to remind ourselves that learning is often frustratingly messy, may take place at inconvenient times and is rarely linear.

To teach and learn without limits is to place trust and empathy first, within a culture of high ambition for all. Essentially, if we believe that labelling children sets limits, then we need to seize 'transformability' as a means to see what might be possible, rather than focusing on perceived deficit. The role of the teacher is complex. We need to recognise that diversity within the community of the classroom is an opportunity and is best embraced as such. Where children are able to build a sense of personal agency, they take the best of what the teacher offers and become intrinsically motivated to learn more. When the school is forgiving of difference and recognises that collectively everyone benefits from other ways of seeing, tolerance, acceptance and mutual respect are built.

To be a professional is to continually appreciate the necessity of building and enhancing one's own expertise. Teaching children like John is difficult. They often rebel against norms and may find it difficult to relate. However, when we can accept that their passions and interests are important, we can learn to respect their individuality and seek every opportunity to challenge and broaden their intellectual development whilst enabling their talents to flourish. If we foster a recognition that difference enriches, rather than demanding conformity at all costs, we model a micro-society within schools that celebrates alternative thinking. In the future, robotic artificial intelligence will only be advanced by those capable of 'thinking the unthinkable'.

When I look back over my career as a teacher, I know that it will be children like John and Arzu that I shall remember the most. Sometimes this will be because I found them a constant challenge, and sometimes it will be with recollections of what it felt like when I saw them achieve something that others may have thought was impossible.

Assessment informs every classroom decision

The official line within the current education inspection framework is that internal tracking data no longer assumes the importance that it used to hold. Some tracking data is necessary, however, to ensure that every child's learning trajectory is noticed. At last, pedagogy and rigorous curriculum design are regaining prominence, with assessment providing information that supports (rather than drives) learning. The importance of teachers being able to articulate not just *what* they are teaching but *why* has been recognised and is to be applauded. In 2010, when the final report of the Cambridge Primary Review was published, Robin Alexander recommended:

> Teachers should be able to give a coherent justification for their practices citing (i) evidence, (ii) pedagogical principle and (iii) educational aim, rather than offering the unsafe defence of compliance with what others expect. Anything else is educationally unsound. (2010)

The current move towards engagement with evidence-informed practice across the profession is beginning to make this vision a reality.

The optimum way of assessing children from the earliest days is to provide a supportive, imaginative learning environment. Within a safe and enticing primary school, children explore, play, build relationships, ask questions and develop a positive self-identity as a learner. The role of the headteacher and their highly qualified teaching team is to help every child to engage in dialogue that supports the development of their learning capacity. This in turn enables the adults to provide stimulus and input that develops the child's understanding. Expert teaching is essential. Talking, expressing opinions, telling stories, listening attentively – these are the fundamental skills of communication that enable learning to take place. Teachers who understand this provide opportunities for every child to rehearse their growing knowledge, share their ideas, explain their thinking, build connections and contribute to collective debate. Children love to aim for their personal best if they are in an environment where challenge has high status.

The alternative school improvement story I have described is explored in *Creating Learning without Limits* (Swann et al., 2012) and the influence of this work across the system is captured in *Assessment for Learning without Limits* (Peacock, 2016). In this chapter, a snapshot of one school and its revolutionary decision to swim against the tide of educational practice has been briefly considered. Although this account relates to one school, we might choose to learn from this that when school leaders are emboldened and informed by evidence and research, it becomes possible to improve the entire system.

References

Alexander, R. J. A. (2004) *Towards dialogic teaching: rethinking classroom talk.* York: Dialogos.

Alexander, R. J. A. (2010) *Children, their world, their education. Final report and recommendations of the Cambridge Primary Review.* London: Routledge.

Hart, S. (1998) 'A sorry tail: ability, pedagogy and educational reform', *British Journal of Educational Studies* 46 (2) pp. 153–168.

Hart, S., Dixon, A., Drummond, M. J. and McIntyre, D. (2004) *Learning without limits.* Maidenhead: Open University Press.

Peacock, A. (2016) *Assessment for learning without limits.* London: Open University Press.

Swann, M., Peacock, A., Hart, S. and Drummond, M. J. (2012) *Creating learning without limits.* Maidenhead: Open University Press.

Author bio-sketch:

Professor Dame Alison Peacock has experience of both secondary and primary teaching. She spent 14 years as a primary headteacher and her work on 'learning without limits' explores alternatives to differentiation and to deterministic notions of fixed ability. She has contributed to this book in a personal capacity drawing upon her many years of teaching experience.

IN PURSUIT OF THE POWERFUL: KNOWLEDGE, KNOWERS AND KNOWING

AND THE IMPACT FOR ASSESSMENT AND FEEDBACK

RUTH POWLEY

Assessment is ubiquitous in education. A quick Google search for 'assessment in education', for example, finds about 989,000,000 results.

Assessment locates our students. It tells us where they are in their learning at a moment in time (to some extent). It tells us where they stand in relation to each other at a moment in time (to some extent). The current importance of this comparative approach looms particularly large in spring 2020 as English schools prepare to rank their students in order to facilitate the awarding of A level and GCSE grades.

In this context, it seems almost sacrilegious to ask:

- Do we need to know so much of what we currently know?
- Can we know what we think we know?
- Might it be more useful to know other things?

Ofsted under Amanda Spielman has brought a welcome refocusing within official circles on the richness of curriculum as a matter of social justice. Her speech at 'The Wonder Years' knowledge curriculum conference critiques 'the consequence of … [curriculum] narrowing[:] … that pupils from disadvantaged backgrounds do lose out on building that body of knowledge that should be every child's entitlement. For that reason, if we really want to reduce economic and social inequality, the place to start is what is taught in the classroom' (Spielman, 2019).

How do current assessment practices fit with building this body of knowledge and encouraging a love of knowledge in our students?

Is there a possibility that by knowing so much (to some extent) about where our students are placed in relation to each other (norm-referenced assessment), we do not focus enough on the importance of what they know and the richness or paucity of their bodies of knowledge (criterion-referenced assessment)?

Additionally, is there a risk that by focusing on 'where students are' in comparison to each other, rather than 'what students know' in terms of acquiring a rich body of knowledge, we run the risk of damaging the encouragement of lifelong learning as the ongoing and self-motivated pursuit of knowledge? Should we therefore be more focused on the 'threshold' (criterion-referenced) model of what we want all our young people to know rather than the comparative and competitive (norm-referenced) model which builds in failure as well as success, and in which half of students must always be below average?

Does it matter more what we know and that, as a society, we have a shared body of powerful knowledge and understanding, or does it matter more that we know what order we are in? And do we consider the impact of the latter on our motivation to pursue the former?

Mike Buscemi's poem 'The Average Child' captures the sense of the average child: 'part of that majority / That hump part of the bell / Who spends his life unnoticed / In an average kind of hell.'

Powerful knowledge: what is it worth assessing?

In *Knowledge and the Future School: Curriculum and Social Justice*, Michael Young and David Lambert sound a clarion call for the teaching of 'better' knowledge: 'the curriculum must be based on the "best knowledge" we have' (2014, p. 71).

This 'powerful' knowledge is not a common core 'fixed in history' (p. 63) but knowledge through subject disciplines (p. 74) that is:

- Distinct from common-sense
- Systematic
- Specialised

In this they can be distinguished from E. D. Hirsch, who refers to the 'communal curriculum' (2016) as the shared knowledge and vocabulary of the nation.

Within the framework of powerful knowledge, we might ask the following questions in deciding what the curriculum should deliver:

Does the curriculum:

- teach the 'best knowledge'?
- explain and enlighten?
- allow students to move beyond their common-sense experiences?
- allow students to understand the world?

Does it, in short, develop 'powerful knowers'?

And what should therefore be assessed?

Does assessment evaluate the extent to which students:

- have acquired the 'best knowledge?
- can explain?
- can move beyond their common-sense experiences?
- can demonstrate understanding of the world?

Assessment within this framework of powerful knowledge requires different questions: more of the 'what' questions of knowledge, as well as the 'how' questions of skills. A framework of powerful knowledge also suggests a criterion-referenced form of assessment. If a student cannot explain or demonstrate understanding, moving beyond their own common-sense experiences of the world, does it matter that their level of incomplete explanation is slightly better than that of another student? If we are aiming to 'stand on the shoulders of giants', is it enough that one student has reached the knees of giants in comparison to another who is still scrabbling at their ankles? Can learning and assessment be 'complete' at this point? Is it sufficient?

Powerful knowers: who is it worth assessing?

Powerful knowledge has the potential to create powerful knowers.

E. D. Hirsch argues that access to parity of knowledge is a 'civil right' (2016). He suggests that 'the achievement gap is chiefly a knowledge gap and a language gap. It can be greatly ameliorated by knowledge-based schooling.' Similarly, Michael Young and David Lambert argue that 'everyone is entitled to a foundation of knowledge' (2014, p. 16):

> Powerful knowledge is the knowledge that pupils have a right of access to that defines their entitlement as pupils. Furthermore, this knowledge has its own rules and criteria which judge all pupils equally, apart from the severely mentally handicapped. That is the starting point for an equal, fair and just system ... Such a curriculum principle takes no account of any differences in perceived or measured ability, disposition, motivation, interest or prior experience of pupils. (pp. 81–82)

The decisions that we take in schools about curricular provision for students are also (inadvertently) decisions about access to parity of knowledge and opportunities for learning which can accumulate over time into significant differences in opportunities to acquire knowledge. In *Becoming a High Expectation Teacher: Raising the Bar*, Christine Rubie-Davies points out that teachers' expectations of students are also reflected in their practice:

> Depending on teachers' beliefs about particular students, they form expectations for their students [that] ... influence their beliefs about what is appropriate pedagogy for the students in their classes. The expectations that teachers form will lead them to plan opportunities to learn for students. These opportunities may be highly differentiated, in that the learning experiences for those considered high-achieving students may be quite different from the learning activities planned for students expected to achieve at lower levels ... Giving a child a label can result in lowered expectations for them. (2014, pp. 15; 21)

The pedagogical choices of teachers, including the way that they assess students and give feedback, can also build in disparity.

In *The Culture of Education*, Jerome Bruner writes that: 'a choice of pedagogy inevitably communicates a conception of the learning process and the learner. Pedagogy is never innocent. It is a medium that carries its own message' (1997, p.63). Brophy (1985) identified 17 teacher pedagogical choices that differed depending on whether the teacher was interacting with high- or low-expectation students, including low-expectation students receiving less challenge in formative assessment and less information in feedback. Differentiated practice for low-expectation students included:

- Less wait time in questioning to ensure a student response
- Less rephrasing or cueing when questioning to ensure a student response
- Fewer opportunities to give public responses
- Less detailed feedback
- Low expectation feedback on quality of task completion

Christine Rubie-Davies suggests that teachers may plan less consistently and give up more easily with students who acquire new knowledge slowly:

> Students for whom teachers have low expectations may experience less consistency in teaching methods than peers. When teachers present a new concept to students, and the students do not immediately grasp the idea, teachers may change the way in which they attempt to teach the concept a second or even third time. This means that students for whom teachers hold low expectations can be exposed to a greater variety of pedagogical approaches than their peers, and this may be confusing for students. (2014, p. 36)

She also points out that students perceived as being of low ability receive a different range of teaching and assessment methods, with a focus on procedures, decoding, reading words without meaningful context and skills-based activities, compared to more emphasis on comprehension and knowledge-based activities for students perceived as being of high ability. E. D. Hirsh suggests that in the US, improvement in the teaching of decoding 'has not produced improvement in the reading comprehension of more demanding texts on more demanding subjects' (2016).

In comparison, Rubie-Davies suggests that 'when teachers believe that all children can learn, the responsibility for student learning shifts to the teacher' (2014, p. 55). In other words, where the focus is on assessment of the *learner*, low expectations can lead to less effective methods of teaching, assessment and feedback. This is removed when the focus is on assessment of the *learning*. Arguably, norm-referenced assessment encourages the assessment of the *learner* within a ranking system, whilst criterion-referencing encourages a focus on assessment of the *learning*.

The expectations that teachers have of students and their placement within a norm-referencing assessment system must also have an effect on students' confidence, sense of academic 'worth' and self-motivation in engaging with powerful knowledge.

Research by McInerney et al. (2012) suggests that academic self-concept, learning strategies and academic achievement have reciprocal relationships with each other. Unsurprisingly, students who believe that they can do well do better than those who believe that they can't. If we don't want a bell curve in student motivation and engagement with rich bodies of knowledge, should we be engaging in different forms of assessment and feedback for our students?

In *Reaching Higher: the Power of Expectations in Schooling*, Rhona Weinstein writes, 'While our categories enable us to see more clearly, they can also blind us. Therein lies the opportunity for limiting or even biased perceptions ... What are the characteristics of individuals and environments in classrooms ... that accentuate or mitigate such self-fulfilling prophecies?' (2002, p. 5). Should we be examining more closely the differentiated assessment and feedback choices that we make in the classroom to ensure that we are not inadvertently and accidentally denying students parity of access to opportunities for learning and the opportunity to become powerful knowers?

Would our students want to know more, if we allowed ourselves to know less?

Powerful knowing: what is it useful to assess?

As a result of my education, I have a particular piece of information. At some point in my teenage years, I was taught to (and can still remember how to) construct a 60-degree angle using a compass. I have not yet had the opportunity to use this piece of information, but I stand prepared should it be required at any point.

This could be described as 'unfinished' knowledge. Unanchored within my knowledge schema it has a floating and random existence, not allowing me to understand the world better. This piece of knowledge is not powerfully known!

A norm-referenced assessment system does not necessarily query the usefulness of my existing state of knowledge or the disuse of 'unfinished' knowledge. It ranks me above someone who cannot construct a 60-degree angle using a compass and below someone who knows more about the underlying structure of this knowledge; and yet, as 'unfinished' knowledge, it is not of use.

Our aim in learning is fluency. Learning is connected to our existing knowledge; it is understood and allows understanding; and it can be applied securely or correctly: perhaps quickly, or with automaticity or precision. In short, fluent learning is powerfully known.

In 'Principles of Instruction', brought to prominence again in 2019 by Tom Sherrington's book *Rosenshine's Principles in Action*, Rosenshine suggests a high success rate during classroom instruction: 'The research suggests that the optimal success rate for fostering student achievement appears to be 80%. A success rate of 80% shows that students are learning the material, and it also shows that the students are challenged' (Rosenshine, 2012, p. 12).

It is presumably our aim in education for students to acquire fluent knowledge and understanding rather than to accumulate the half-known, incompletely understood and quickly forgotten. If Mark is confused about an element of the learning, is it sufficient that he understands it with slightly fewer errors and misconceptions than Simon? Criterion-referenced assessment throws down a gauntlet to teachers that all students should have high levels of knowledge and understanding of the content that they are being instructed in. It seems reasonable to use Rosenshine's suggestion of 80% as a benchmark for this. If our assessment is not focused on all students gaining 80% success rates in their learning, then how can we foster both student achievement in their learning tasks and student perceptions of success within learning, which in turn increase motivation for engagement with knowledge acquisition? Without this level of success, can learning be powerfully known and is there a risk that, as educators, we are too easily satisfied?

Undoubtedly, this presents a challenge if we are endeavoring to give students access to parity of curriculum experience – and this chapter does not attempt to present easy answers to this conundrum – but it does suggest that our focus should be more on creating similar successful, powerful and rewarding learning experiences for our students and less on measuring differences that can demotivate and disengage.

Norm-referenced assessment has its own ending in the relative performance of the learner, whereas criterion-referenced assessment implicitly poses questions about the sufficiency of the learning. If the result is not 80%, then the learning is not powerful, successful (or 'finished'). This then also guides our feedback and marking, which are directed to the goal of achieving learning that is 80% successful.

Powerful knowing: when is it useful to assess?

In *Powerful Pedagogy: Teach Better Quicker* (Powley, 2018), I examine the stages of learning (p. 118) from initial understanding, through transfer to and storage within long-term memory (storage strength), and finally to effective recall (retrieval strength). Assessment is necessary during each of these stages.

What seems of particular interest when assessing for permanent learning is the differentiation within assessment between:

1. That which was never known
2. That which was never understood
3. That which was once understood but has been forgotten

Is it possible that a sharper focus on these distinctions would allow us to hone our medium-term summative assessment practices, with most medium-term summative assessment focused on addressing category 3?

Assessment using low-stakes testing is currently *en vogue* as the most effective way of ensuring that learning has actually been learned (as opposed to learning which has been forgotten). As Karpicke points out, retrieval does not merely assess learning: it also enhances it because 'learning is altered by the act of retrieval itself' (2012). Testing strengthens both long-term memory (storage strength) and retrieval pathways (retrieval strength) as well as interrupting the 'forgetting' process. Learning therefore becomes more durable, particularly when testing is effortful and occurs in regular spaced sessions over a course of study. Rawson and Dunlosky (2012) point out that in retrieval practice, the provision of correction through corrective feedback or reteaching is particularly important in order to remove errors and misconceptions.

If our aim is to embed powerful knowledge and prevent lost learning, rather than intelligence ranking, then regular ongoing low-stakes criterion-based assessment built into curriculum sequences will be of value in ensuring that learning can remain powerfully known rather than being transient and ephemeral.

Powerful knowers: how do we ensure access to assessment?

TIMSS (Trends in International Mathematics and Science Study) and PISA (Programme for International Student Assessment) assess pupil achievement across a number of countries in different ways. TIMSS is an analysis of mathematics and science curricula across participating countries, assessing pupils' knowledge and skills. Questions tend to be short and focused on facts and processes. In comparison, PISA assesses the application of skills to real-life problems, testing functional skills that students have acquired in the format of real-word problems with longer text and instructions. Therefore, students are doubly assessed, for their reading comprehension as well as their mathematical or scientific understanding. This gives an example of the underlying knowledge and skills that students require in order to be powerful knowers and to enjoy successful experiences of learning and assessment.

In *Closing the Vocabulary Gap* (2018), Alex Quigley points out that reading comprehension requires understanding of 95–98% of the text (p. 7). He suggests that therefore we should aim for students to leave school with a 'word hoard' of 50,000 words (p. 6) – a criterion-referenced rather than norm-referenced standard. E. D. Hirsh suggests that the average reading score of students is vital, predicting 'students' college and career readiness and their later economic success' (2016). He decries 'too much time … being spent on test preparation in early [US] grades, and too little time … being spent on gaining the wide knowledge required for a broad vocabulary'. This is a criticism that may be equally true of the narrowed English curriculum.

E. D. Hirsch points out the power of vocabulary in 'A Wealth of Words' (2013): 'Vocabulary size is a convenient proxy for a whole range of educational attainments and abilities – not just skill in reading, writing, listening and speaking, but also general knowledge of science, history and the arts.'

The acquisition of fluent or powerful reading skills undoubtedly improves acquisition of knowledge and ability to access assessment. However, whilst the focus on reading fluency is an important one, two other competencies are worth highlighting as part of increasing students' access to assessments:

1. **Writing fluency:** Generation Z students get far fewer opportunities to practise the mechanics of handwriting than earlier generations. It is therefore probable that lack of automaticity and fluency in this skill adds extraneous cognitive load for 'reluctant writers'.
2. **Attention:** As explained by Weinstein and Sumeracki (2019), attention is notoriously hard to pin down. However, researchers have proposed that about half the time, students are not paying attention to what the teacher is saying in class. Studies suggest that mind-wandering varies widely between students and, unsurprisingly, is negatively related to comprehension, whilst in tests it can lead to poor

time management and exam failure (pp. 56–60). Three theories have attempted to account for differences in attention spans:

i.   Differences in working memory capacity

ii. Differences in processing speed

iii. Differences in attentional control

Powerful knowledge: what can we know?

Opportunity cost refers to the loss of other alternatives when one alternative is chosen.

In *Responsive Teaching* (2018), Harry Fletcher-Wood warns against assessment which is 'superficially precise, but practically incoherent' without reference to what students actually know. Tom Sherrington points out that 'grades themselves do not actually tell us much at all about what students know or can do at a level that is actionable' (2017, p. 117).

Numbers and grades can be superficially seductive, suggesting objectivity and certainty. However, in assessment they can also be flawed and erroneous. Ofqual's *Marking consistency metrics* (2018) found that the probability of students receiving a 'definitive' qualification grade varied across subjects from 0.96 for a mathematics qualification, to 0.52 for an English language and literature qualification, with similarly low figures for history, business studies and sociology. For subjects in which long extended responses might be regarded as an important element of assessment, a degree of reliability will always be lost.

Daisy Christodolou (2016, pp. 113–137; 193) warns that exam-based assessments can also be difficult to use for formative purposes because:

- A summative examination merely samples from the subject domain rather than covering all of it.
- The complexity of many exam questions makes it hard to make accurate diagnostic formative inferences.
- Grading systems for summative exams are intended to measure big subject domains and are therefore not sufficiently sensitive to provide reliable formative feedback on smaller domains.

Do the benefits of grading outweigh the disadvantages, and do grades create more powerful knowers?

Powerful knowing: powerful feedback

The feedback loop is the part of a system in which some portion of the system's output is used as input/decision-making for future operations. In *Leadership for Teaching Learning* (2016), Dylan Wiliam points out that assessment can be defined as formative or summative based on the inference to be drawn from it (p. 107):

- Summative assessment relates to assessment of the current or future performance of the student.
- Formative assessment relates to the planning of future teaching activities.

In other words, formative assessment is part of the feedback loop in teaching.

It is perhaps unhelpful that feedback has become particularly associated with marking when formative or 'responsive' teaching can be more helpful than marking. Hattie and Timperley (2007) point out that where students lack sufficient knowledge, further teaching is more effective than feedback; therefore, if formative assessment demonstrates that learning has had less than 80% success, the teacher may be better employed in reteaching the content 'live' than laboriously correcting misconceptions by writing corrections on a student's work.

If our aim is powerful *learning* that achieves a success rate of 80% success, then assessment and feedback should aim to:

- Identify current rates of success through effective formative assessment.
- Plan effective teacher and student actions to increase the success rate to 80%.

Rosenshine's 'Principles of Instruction' (2012) seem sensible here with their focus on:

- Presentation of new knowledge in small steps (linked to prior learning) with guided student practice and effective formative assessment to provide feedback loop

- Provision of scaffolds and models of success
- Monitoring of independent practice as part of feedback loop
- Regular review as part of feedback loop

Conclusion

Assessment is not an end in itself but a tool.

This chapter suggests that the aim of education should be the pursuit of the powerful through:

- The delivery of powerful knowledge
- The development of powerful learners
- A focus on powerful learning

These aims may lead us to question and reconsider the way that we employ assessment and feedback to ensure that they are sufficient, or at least more effective:

- The delivery of powerful knowledge: if we focus on giving students rich bodies of knowledge, does this change the way that we assess and give feedback? Might it be more useful to test the delivery of our powerful curriculum through criterion-referenced testing?
- The development of powerful learners: do the ways that we construct our curricula and pedagogy allow all learners to access powerful learning? Do we provide enough of the tools to access powerful learning? Does what we know through a norm-referenced assessment system discourage the development of a larger number of powerful learners? Indeed, with the errors built into a grading system, do we even know what we think we know?
- A focus on powerful learning: do we focus sufficiently on complete learning? If we work to 80% success rates, does this change the way that we teach, assess and give feedback, focusing us more on the quality of the learning and less on the quality of the learner?

Have our assessments focused on differences of learner, where they should have focused on similarities of powerful learning? And, if yes, what should we do next?

References

Brophy, J. E. (1985) 'Teacher-student interaction' in Dusek, J. B., Hall, V. C. and Meyer, W. J. (eds) *Teacher expectancies*. Hillsdale, NJ: Lawrence Erlbaum, pp. 303–327.

Bruner, J. (1997) *The culture of education*. Cambridge, MA: Harvard University Press.

Fletcher-Wood, H. (2018) *Responsive teaching: cognitive science and formative assessment in practice*. Abingdon: Routledge.

Hattie, J. and Timperley, H. (2007) 'The power of feedback', *Review of Educational Research* 77 (1) pp. 81–112.

Hirsch, E. D. (2013) 'A wealth of words', *City Journal* 23 (1). Retrieved from: www.bit.ly/2WScZID

Hirsch, E. D. (2016) *Why knowledge matters: rescuing our children from failed educational theories*. Cambridge, MA: Harvard Education Press.

Karpicke, J. D. (2012) 'Retrieval-based learning: active retrieval promotes meaningful learning', *Current Directions in Psychological Science* 21 (3) pp. 157–163.

McInerney, D. M., Cheng, R. W., Mok, M. M. C. and Lam, A. K. H. (2012) 'Academic self-concept and learning strategies direction of effect on student academic achievement', *Journal of Advanced Academics* 23 (3) pp. 249–269.

Ofqual (2018) *Marking consistency metrics*. Coventry: Ofqual.

Powley, R. (2018) *Powerful pedagogy: teach better quicker*. Abingdon: Routledge.

Quigley, A. (2018) *Closing the vocabulary gap*. Abingdon: Routledge.

Rawson, K. A. and Dunlosky, J. (2012) 'When is practice testing most effective for improving the durability and efficiency of student learning?', *Educational Psychology Review* 24 (3) pp. 419–435.

Rosenshine, B. (2012) 'Principles of instruction: research-based strategies that all teachers should know', *American Educator* 36 (1) pp. 12–19, 39.

Rubie-Davies, C. (2014) *Becoming a high expectation teacher: raising the bar*. Abingdon: Routledge.

Sherrington, T. (2017) *The learning rainforest: great teaching in great classrooms.* Woodbridge: John Catt Educational.

Spielman, A. (2019) [Keynote speech], *'The wonder years' curriculum conference,* Pimlico Academy, London, 26 January. Retrieved from www.bit.ly/3bTdYN0

Weinstein, R. S. (2002) *Reaching higher: the power of expectations in schooling.* Cambridge, MA: Harvard University Press.

Weinstein, Y. and Sumeracki, M. (2019) *Understanding how we learn: a visual guide.* Abingdon: Routledge.

Wiliam, D. (2016) *Leadership for teaching learning.* West Palm Beach, FL: Learning Sciences International.

Young, M. and Lambert, D. (2014) *Knowledge and the future school: curriculum and social justice.* London: Bloomsbury.

Author bio-sketch:

Ruth Powley is currently deputy headteacher at Wilmslow High School in Cheshire. A keen advocate for teaching as a research-informed profession, she is the author of the *Love Learning Ideas* website and *Powerful Pedagogy*, a book examining how knowledge of pedagogy allows us to teach better quicker.

STRENGTH IN NUMBERS: OPERATIONALISING A NETWORK-WIDE ASSESSMENT MODEL

RICH DAVIES

Data has experienced something of a reputational rollercoaster during the past few years. For a while, it seemed untouchable, as the DfE, Ofsted and others treated exam results and even internal assessments with almost religious reverence. But then the doubt set in. Between the DfE's *Making data work* report (Department for Education, 2018), which called on schools to fundamentally rethink how they used data, and Ofsted's radical new inspection framework (Ofsted, 2019), which essentially U-turned the inspectorate's approach to data, many within the educational establishment have begun to question the purpose of assessment data. But, as someone who welcomed both of these interventions, my own perspective on what this purpose is remains unchanged.

Throughout my six years at Ark Schools, a large network of primary and secondary academies serving disadvantaged communities, we based our approach to assessment data on the following three axioms:

- Improved outcomes are supported by informed actions.
- Informed actions are supported by insightful analyses.
- Insightful analyses are supported by accurate data.

As such, the primary purpose of the network's assessment data was (and still is) to inform the teaching and leadership actions that will help improve student outcomes.

I joined Ark around the time that national curriculum levels were being abolished. This change undoubtedly led to much confusion and miscoordination within the sector, but it also provided an ideal opportunity for schools – and particularly networks of schools – to design and implement new assessment models that could better fulfil this purpose of informing teaching and leadership actions.

Fortunately for Ark (and me), I was not the only new recruit that term. An up-and-coming educationalist named Daisy Christodoulou had just finished writing her first book, *Seven Myths About Education*, and was now aiming to design a research-informed assessment model that leveraged the advantages of belonging to a large network of schools.

Daisy has already published the fruits of this research in her second book, *Making Good Progress?* So, rather than plagiarise that superior work here, I am going to focus this essay on how we went about operationalising this assessment model across our network.

Assessment principles

Ark's network-wide assessment model was continuously developed and refined over the years, but the following five principles remained intact throughout:

Different assessments for different purposes

Formative and summative assessments are fundamentally different tools that should not be conflated or used interchangeably.

Formative assessments involve setting tasks/questions that check for highly specific knowledge and skills. Meanwhile, summative questions are multi-faceted and check for the retention and application of a broader knowledge and skills base from throughout a course. Formative assessment data helps show what each student can and can't do at a granular level, while summative assessment data helps show how well students are progressing more generally. Formative assessments inform teachers' immediate next steps with each student, while summative assessments better inform longer-term and/or larger-scale planning.

Other important types of assessment include baseline assessments, which help establish students' start points prior to a course of study, and normative assessments, which help compare students' progress against that of a relevant national cohort.

For Ark, operationalising this principle meant working with all of our teachers to (re)define what we were doing to assess our students, as well as explicitly stating why we were doing it.

Frequent, specific, non-graded formative assessments

Formative assessment is a continuous process, but it is not appropriate or useful to grade students using GCSE scales, sub-levels or any other labels that imply a position along the national bell curve.

In one of the many vivid analogies employed in *Making Good Progress?*, Daisy invites her readers to imagine a marathon runner measuring their weight training or circuit exercises in hours rather than in kilograms or reps, her point being that just because the final race will be timed, that doesn't make time the only valuable metric while training. Similarly, just because students will eventually receive a GCSE grade in English, that doesn't mean that correctly using a comma in a year 7 haiku could or should be translated into a grade.

To be clear, the formative data generated by checking if a student can properly apply some recently taught knowledge or skill is still extremely important, but encoding this data as a grade is at best pointless and at worst misleading.

For Ark, operationalising this principle meant (re)training all teachers in high-quality formative assessment practice and (re)setting expectations around what – if any – formative data could or should be collected.

Common summative assessments

The most consistent means of comparing students' understanding of a subject or topic involves asking them all the exact same questions.

Criterion-based approaches are much more open to inconsistent teacher interpretation, which ultimately undermines their utility. For example, the criterion 'can compare two fractions' could be interpreted as being able to compare 3/7 with 5/6 (which 90% of 14-year-olds can do), but could also be interpreted as being able to compare 5/7 with 5/9 (which only 15% of 14-year-olds can do) (Wiliam, 2014). Even two very similar interpretations of the same criterion (e.g. 11+3 vs 3+11) can lead to very different outcomes, as can different sequencing and/or framing of questions.

For Ark, operationalising this principle meant developing and implementing network-wide summative assessments across most subjects.

Cumulative tests for summative assessments

Cumulative tests sample from all the knowledge that has been taught to date, but not any content that has yet to be taught.

If your summative assessment only tests what has been taught most recently, you cannot be confident that students have fully retained and incorporated content that was taught previously. Conversely, if your summative assessment includes content that has not yet been taught, you are not really assessing learning, but rather an unpredictable blend of raw intelligence, cultural capital and luck.

For Ark, operationalising this principle meant ensuring that all network-wide summative assessments reflected consistently sequenced progression along a common curriculum.

Year-group based referencing for summative assessments
It is usually neither appropriate nor useful to measure students in different year-groups against a common scale. Measuring students relative to their peers within the same year-group is both simpler and more meaningful.

During the era of national curriculum levels, schools across the country formulated fictional 'flight paths' charting expected trajectories of sub-levels over time. Following the abolition of levels, many schools simply resurrected this approach with new labels (e.g. GCSE grades), but these new flight paths were every bit as imaginary as their predecessors. For example, awarding all year 7 students U grades in History because that's how they would all currently score on a final GCSE paper is the very antithesis of useful summative assessment data.

Year-group-based referencing removes the need for these flight paths. If you can say that a student is currently performing among the top 10% nationally for their year-group, you don't need to illustrate how that might translate into future performance.

For Ark, operationalising this principle meant (re)calibrating our summative grading and associated systems to an 'age-related' model, where students were always compared against an estimated national distribution for their own year-group – be that reception, year 6 or year 13.

Operational enablers
Putting these principles into practice involved many years of coordinated effort across multiple central and school-based teams. I should probably state up front that two of the most important enablers – professional development and assessment writing – had relatively little to do with me. Over the years, Ark's professional development team went about embedding high-quality formative

practice among thousands of classroom teachers, while Ark's expert assessment authors created high-quality test materials that have since been taken by thousands of students.

Meanwhile, I focused on leveraging consistency, scale and technology to develop the following five areas.

Aligned inputs

Assessment is intrinsically linked to the underlying curriculum, so if you are going to align on one, it is only logical to also align on the other. At Ark, we talked about 'curriculum' at three broad levels: macro-curriculum (i.e. the time spent teaching each subject); design architecture (i.e. the knowledge and skills covered within each subject); and delivery architecture (i.e. the resources and approaches used to teach each subject).

From an assessment perspective, it felt most important to align on macro-curriculum and design architecture. This meant that the same knowledge was being taught via the same volume of teaching over the same period of time across all schools. In order to align on macro-curriculum, we developed a 'base curriculum', which outlined the expected entitlement for all students. Schools could sometimes deviate from this curriculum on an exceptional basis, but only with a clear rationale. Meanwhile, Ark Curriculum Partnerships (ACP) was developed to align the network around best practice design architecture. This new venture brought together Ark's existing Mathematics and English Mastery programmes, as well as initiating Science and Geography Mastery pilots and driving the establishment of network-wide subject communities across most other subjects.

While these various ACP programmes also generated significant delivery architecture collateral, less focus was placed on ensuring network-wide alignment along this dimension. In practice, this meant that all schools and teachers in the network were expected to cover the same content over time, but the way they delivered that content was still primarily treated as a local decision.

One practical implication of this approach was around summative assessment frequency, which dropped from six or more times per year to just once or twice per year. Essentially, by aligning on macro-curriculum and design architecture, but less so on delivery architecture, we had confidence that the same content would be taught in each school by the end of each year, but not necessarily by the end of any given week or half term. This naturally limited how often we could administer our network-wide assessments, since they were only meaningful when we could compare like with like.

This commitment to comparing like with like also drove us to better align on assessment framing, preparation, test conditions and marking/moderation. Prior to introducing common assessments, we found that some schools framed internal assessment windows as high stakes while others kept things much more low key. Similarly, some schools explicitly prepared students for internal assessments while others did not. And in terms of exam conditions, an end-of-year assessment could be taken under strict invigilation in one school but under normal lesson conditions in another. Ultimately, even with our curriculum and assessment cycle aligned, we could not hope to compare like with like without aligning on these additional factors too. We also invested in training teachers to mark consistently and scheduled network-wide moderation sessions within each assessment window.

Efficient data collection
Collecting data will always incur some kind of cost, but since the data being collected has potential benefit , any decisions that influence collection need to be made on a 'cost vs benefit' basis.

One such decision is the frequency of summative assessments. Reducing frequency clearly reduces the cost of data collection, but how much benefit gets relinquished as a result? In Ark's case, the limits of curriculum alignment somewhat capped the potential benefits of assessing more than once or twice per year. However, even in networks with more aligned delivery architecture, leaders should still question just how much marginal benefit each additional assessment window can really provide, especially when compared with the marginal cost incurred – not just in terms of data collection workload, but also lost lesson time and overall disruption to the flow of the school year.

We also applied this 'cost vs benefit' approach when shifting from capturing grade bands to raw marks. Grades can always be derived from raw marks, but the same cannot be said in reverse. As such, while the cost is broadly the same either way, the potential benefit of raw mark capture generally exceeds that of grade band capture.

However, while it may always be better to collect raw marks rather than grades, deciding between collecting *total* raw marks vs *individual question level* marks is less clear cut. Collecting question-level data is clearly the higher-cost option, but the potential benefit may sometimes justify this investment. Resolving this trade-off ultimately depends on how the data will actually be used to inform follow-up activities.

For example, using question-level data to identify a class or school's relative topic strengths could generate positive value by helping focus future resource allocation, but only if there is scope to actually focus resources along these lines. We therefore limited our question-level collection to the subjects and year groups which had most capacity to act upon the resultant insights. In all other cases, we restricted data collection to total or paper-level raw mark entry.

However, when we did choose to collect question-level summative data, we discouraged teachers from misusing this data to identify apparent misconceptions among individual students. Summative test questions are not usually designed for this purpose, so incorrect answers cannot necessarily be attributed to particular misconceptions, tempting though this may seem (Benyohai, 2018). This is ultimately the role of formative assessment, where the questions can be fine-tuned to root out specific misconceptions.

Finally, it's worth conceding that while the cost of data collection should obviously be minimised wherever possible, there will likely always be some workload associated with collecting assessment data. But despite this inevitability, decisions can still be made to distribute this workload more efficiently.

For example, while there are benefits to the same teacher(s) marking multiple scripts, this doesn't mean that these same teachers need to be the ones manually entering the resultant data. Better still, in some cases students can take tests online, with automated calculation and transfer of raw marks. Admittedly, during my time at Ark, we struggled to make online testing technically feasible in most schools, but we did manage to reduce marking and data-entry workload through other technological solutions, like online comparative judgement.

Meaningful grading

Raw marks can show us how many questions each student got right or wrong on a given test, but this information is of limited value without gauging the difficulty of these questions. On the other hand, converting these raw marks into some kind of grade can help us approximate where a student resides along the national distribution. In isolation, this may not seem much more useful than raw marks, but it becomes increasingly more useful when we can compare it with other related data points. For example, if a student appears to move significantly upwards or downwards along this national distribution, that is useful to know. Similarly, if a student's position on the national distribution appears to diverge significantly between different subjects, that is also useful information.

Of course, individual student data can be very 'noisy', but this noise becomes increasingly attenuated as data gets aggregated across multiple students. As such, approximating a class, year or school's *average* position along the national distribution can help inform school and network leaders' periodic decisions around where to invest the scarce resources at their disposal.

But why did we at Ark choose to encode this data as 9–1 or A*–E grades? One simple answer was pragmatism. The national distribution was already broken down into these well recognised (but somewhat arbitrary) segments at the end of each key stage, so it made things less convoluted if we used the same conventions. Furthermore, if we didn't encode this data as grades at a network level, schools and teachers would most likely have done something similar anyway. As such, by approaching these approximations at a network-level, we could ensure consistency, so when two heads of maths talked about their grade 9 students, they were both talking about students that we believed to be performing within the top 3% nationally.

In order to develop this network-wide approach, we relied on consistency, scale and technology. When all students across the network took the same blind test, at the same time, under the same conditions, having covered the same content, we had a sample of more than 3000 students per assessment (e.g. for year 9 geography). We then developed systems to capture raw marks for each of these students, providing us with a network distribution curve.

Next, we used a student's position on our *network* distribution to approximate their position along the *national* distribution. We did this by:

- Starting with the final grade distribution from a relevant historic network cohort (e.g. the previous year's year 11 GCSE Geography)
- Breaking this historic cohort's grade distribution down by prior attainment (e.g. KS2 or, better still, a nationally standardised test taken during KS3)
- Re-weighting the grade distribution of the historic cohort (e.g. the previous year's year 11 GCSE G eography) using the prior attainment of the cohort that was now being assessed (e.g. Year 9 geography)

For example, if the previous year's year 11 GCSE Geography cohort had the following grade distribution:

Grade	7+	4–6	1–3	U
Percentage of historic cohort	10%	50%	30%	10%

and this distribution broke down by prior attainment as follows:

Percentage of historic cohort	Prior attainment	7+	4–6	1–3	U
15%	Highest	50%	40%	10%	0%
15%	High	10%	80%	10%	0%
20%	Upper Mid	5%	75%	15%	5%
20%	Lower Mid	0%	60%	30%	10%
15%	Low	0%	25%	60%	15%
15%	Lowest	0%	10%	60%	30%
100%	All	10%	50%	30%	10%

but the year 9 geography cohort that we were now assessing had the following (higher) prior attainment profile:

Percentage of historic cohort	Prior attainment
20%	Highest
20%	High
20%	Upper Mid
15%	Lower Mid
15%	Low
10%	Lowest

then re-weighting last year's year 11 GCSE Geography grade distribution using our year 9 geography cohort's prior attainment profile yielded the following approximate grade distribution:

Percentage of historic cohort	Prior attainment	7+	4–6	1–3	U
20%	Highest	50%	40%	10%	0%
20%	High	10%	80%	10%	0%
20%	Upper Mid	5%	75%	15%	5%
15%	Lower Mid	0%	60%	30%	10%
15%	Low	0%	25%	60%	15%
10%	Lowest	0%	10%	60%	30%
100%	**All**	**13%**	**53%**	**26%**	**8%**

In other words, the top 10% of last year's year 11 GCSE Geography cohort achieved a grade 7 or better, but our year 9 geography cohort had slightly higher prior attainment than they did, so we could approximate that the top 13% of this new cohort were positioned within the grade 7/8/9 segment of the national bell curve. Similarly, we could approximate that the next highest scoring 53% were positioned within the grade 4/5/6 segment of the national curve, and so on for the remaining segments.

We further refined this approach by interpolating additional grade breakdowns within each segment (e.g. grade 4 vs 5 vs 6), and also made appropriate adjustments for tiered papers and/or inter-related subjects like Combined Science and 'Triple Science' . We also made occasional adjustments to account for any anticipated sample biases (though the act of re-weighting based on prior attainment already addressed this to some extent). But the general approach was as described above and was essentially very similar to what exam boards call 'comparable outcomes'.

To be clear, this approach relied on the assumption that *network-wide* performance within a given subject remained stable over time (after adjusting for changes in prior attainment profiles). This assumption generally holds true at a national level, but is usually not the case at individual school level. As such, the extent to which this assumption holds for any given network will depend on its overall size and general stability. Ark was pretty big and fairly stable (at a network level), so it held relatively well in our case.

However, the validity of this assumption was actually less critical than some might assume. While it would of course have been satisfying to get these network-to-national approximations spot on each time, this wouldn't necessarily have changed our insights or the actions that followed from them.

After all, the explicit purpose of this summative data was to inform school and network leaders' decisions, which mostly involved determining where to invest the scarce resources at their disposal. In other words, this data was fundamentally about *prioritisation*, which is – by definition – a relativist exercise. As such, so long as it helped us understand how students, classes and schools were performing relative to each other, it was not necessarily that important for us to know their exact positions along the national curve.

This meant that the most useful summative assessment data we had at our disposal was each student's network percentile ranking, while the grades that we derived from these rankings were simply the pragmatic but imperfect translation of these rankings into the common language of GCSE (or A level, SATs etc.) grades. While this statement may surprise or even concern some, it need not be a problem, so long as we all understand what these grades really meant and, perhaps more importantly, what they did not.

These grades were consistently derived *approximations* of our students' current performance relative to their national peers. They were a way to quantify differences between class or school averages in a language that most teachers were familiar with. They were even potential indicators of large differences between individual students' current performance and/or large swings in an individual student's performance over time.

However, these grades were not accurate predictions of any *individual* student's future performance. Nor could they ever have been, since student progress trajectories are infamously variable (Treadaway, 2015) and even final GCSE grades are not as reliable as many assume them to be (Sherwood, 2019). They were not even a precise way to quantify differences between individual students' current performance or in an individual student's performance over time, since underlying differences could either be amplified or hidden depending on their proximity to grade boundaries. And this is before we even consider the various forms of measurement error that might have influenced any individual student's apparent performance. As a result of this uncertainty, we usually discussed individual student grades using a ±1 range, but class/school averages with more precision.

But most of all, these grades did not (and, indeed, could not) tell teachers what their students had and hadn't learned. This was never their purpose, but it was the explicit purpose of formative assessment, which is why Ark invested so much effort into developing teachers' formative assessment practices in concert with the work on summative assessment described in this essay.

Actionable analysis

My role at Ark involved analysing our assessment data to help inform network-wide actions. However, it was even more important that our thousands of teachers and leaders were empowered to perform their own analyses to inform myriad local-level actions.

In schools up and down the country, teachers and school leaders are routinely asked to analyse their assessment data, but such requests often fail to define the purpose or scope of these analyses. Even relatively simple data sets can be analysed in multiple different ways, so aiming to simply 'analyse' them without first defining the actions you wish to inform or the insights required to guide these actions is a recipe for so-called 'analysis paralysis'.

To help avoid this, we encouraged teachers and leaders to frame their assessment analyses in terms of:

- **What** needed to be measured – e.g. attainment, progress or gaps vs expectations (n.b. These could be subject-specific or cross-subject measures – e.g. Attainment 8.)
- **How** this could be quantified – e.g. averages, thresholds, distribution patterns or correlations
- **Who** should be compared – e.g. schools, departments, classes, characteristic groups, or individual students (n.b. 'Trend' analyses involved comparing various groups against themselves, albeit at different points in time.)

The most useful what/how/who combination to use for any given analysis mostly depended on the potential decisions and actions available to the analyst or audience.

For example, for a departmental leader who could decide which classes to provide most support to, they could define their analysis as follows:

- **What:** Progress (i.e. change in attainment since a relevant baseline)
- **How:** Average (perhaps sense-checked with a distribution pattern)
- **Who:** Classes

Meanwhile, for a network leader who could decide which subjects' assessments to invest in improving, they could instead analyse:

- **What:** Final exam grades vs latest summative assessments
- **How:** Correlation
- **Who:** Subject

At this point, it's worth stressing that all comparisons between different 'who' groups should ideally be tested for statistical significance in order to avoid over-interpretation. Statistical significance depends not only on the values being compared, but also the standard deviations (i.e. spread) and sample sizes of each group. In general, the smaller the standard deviations and the larger the sample sizes, the more likely that the difference will be statistically significant.

For example, if we are comparing the attainment of two classes with the following values:

- Class A: average = 75, standard deviation = 20, sample size = 10
- Class B: average = 70, standard deviation = 18, sample size = 12

we can only be less than 50% confident that class B actually has lower average attainment than class A.

Meanwhile, if we compare two other classes with the following values:

- Class C: average = 75, standard deviation = 10, sample size = 35
- Class D: average = 70, standard deviation = 9, sample size = 36

we can now be around 97% confident that class D actually has lower average attainment than class C.

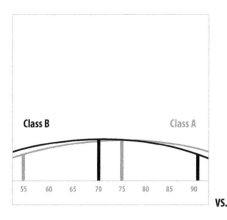

VS.

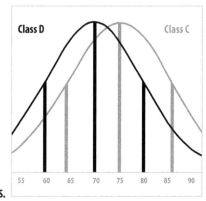

While calculating these values involves navigating a hefty formula as well as a large lookup table, there are plenty of online calculators available to help lighten the cognitive load.

But statistical insignificance is not the only misinterpretation worth sense-checking analyses for. Another frequent offender is known as 'sampling on the dependent variable'. How many times have you come across an analytical approach along the lines of: 'We looked at the top ten performers and determined what they had in common'?

This approach sounds quite logical until you ask yourself whether the bottom ten performers also had those things in common with their higher-performing counterparts. But if nobody looked at the bottom ten (and everyone else, for that matter), you simply cannot know. To help avoid this issue, we ensured that all our standard analyses always showed our high performers, low performers, and everyone in between.

Another common cause of misinterpretation is known as 'what you see is all there is'. Imagine a school leader hands you a chart that appears to show girls outperform boys in English and maths . Before you know it, you've signed off an initiative to better support boys. Except, if you had dug deeper, you would have found that the girls only outperform the boys in English, not maths. Furthermore, the prior attainment of the girls was much, much higher than the boys, so the boys have actually made more progress in both subjects. Why didn't it occur to you to perform these deeper analyses? Because the initial narrative was coherent and compelling. To counter this common problem , we worked to establish a healthy culture of challenge and support across the network, where no narrative – no matter how coherent or compelling – was simply accepted without further probing. One additional advantage of establishing this kind of culture is that it normalises challenge, so teachers and leaders are potentially less likely to feel defensive when their interpretation of the data is sense-checked and expanded upon.

The final common misinterpretation that we proactively worked to counter was confirmation bias . You have a favourite intervention strategy which you'd like to be rolled out across the school. So you select ten students, administer the intervention, then use their (mostly improved) results to justify your school-wide roll-out. Did you test out any alternative interventions? Or check if there was any other reason why these students' results (mostly) improved? Maybe you did, but many don't. To counter this pernicious bias, we encouraged leaders and teachers to test alternative interpretations and make genuine efforts to disprove their initial hypotheses. These various sense-checks do not come naturally to most analysts, but – like most other good habits – they can eventually become habitual through deliberate practice.

Tailored systems

Most of the operational enablers that I've described above – from data collection, to grading, to analysis – have implicitly depended on systems in order to work at scale. Indeed, any assessment model that spans multiple subjects, cohorts and schools needs scalable underlying systems in order to maximise insights while minimising workload. At Ark, we developed our own systems in house, allowing us to define network-wide assessments, create and deploy mark sheets, consolidate raw marks, calculate grades and analyse results. This approach will not be feasible for most schools, but there are an increasing number of commercial solutions that can help schools perform some or – if combined into a coherent ecosystem – all of these tasks.

Whether systems are developed in house or configured from off-the-shelf solutions, the important thing we learned was that these systems had to be designed/configured based on the needs of the assessment model and not the other way around. Beyond this, our other main design principle was 'enter once; use many times' – i.e. once a data point had been entered into a system, it did not need to be re-entered again into any other system or document. To achieve this, we mapped out the 'journey' of each data point from inception to analysis. We then pre-programmed all associated logic and calculations into the underlying system, as well as automating feeds between systems for all relevant characteristic and/or prior-attainment data.

We also worked hard to embed data visualisation throughout our systems, since our brains are generally much better (and quicker) at deriving insights from visuals than from tables (Few, 2009).

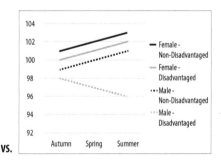

		Autumn	Spring	Summer
Female	Non-Disadvantaged	101	102	103
	Disadvantaged	100	101	102
Male	Non-Disadvantaged	99	100	101
	Disadvantaged	98	97	96

VS.

However, since even well-designed visualisations can seem complex upon first viewing, we strived to maintain visual consistency throughout our systems. In general, we found that our teachers and leaders were quite capable of understanding relatively complex visualisations, provided they didn't need to re-learn to read each new dashboard. With this in mind, we used the same layouts, chart-types, colour schemes and terminology across all year groups, subjects and measure types. These visualisations were also consistently interactive, so hovering over or clicking on a data point always helped furthered one's line of inquiry in an intuitive and predictable way.

One final but vitally important consideration around systems is, of course, data security. Student data is sensitive and must be handled with the utmost care and respect. Any systems should obviously be reviewed in advance from a data security perspective. However, given that most data breaches result from human (rather than system) error, it is probably even more important to review your data-related processes and behaviours (CybSafe, 2020). Once again, considering the 'journey' of each data point should help anticipate potential vulnerabilities. Where does the data reside at different stages? Who has access to it? When is it most likely to be copied, exported or printed? In some cases, system features can be put in place to minimise these risks, but the best defence is to embed rigid procedures for data handling and a strong culture of respect for data security.

Consistency, scale and technology

This account only scratches the surface of the many challenges we experienced while operationalising Ark's assessment model across nearly forty schools. Nevertheless, I hope that the main themes of this essay – i.e. the importance of consistency, scale and technology – will resonate with other network leaders working with assessment data.

- **Consistency:** Aligned definitions, assessments, calendars, measures, visualisations and analyses
- **Scale:** Large sample sizes, central administration, targeted resourcing and cross-school collaboration
- **Technology:** 'Enter once, use many times', cross-system data-feeds, automated logic and interactive analytics

I continue to believe that assessment data's main purpose is to inform teaching and leadership actions, demonstrating which students need what teacher support, which teachers need what leadership support and which leaders need what network support. As such, it remains vital that schools and networks keep doing all they can to ensure their assessment data is truly fit for this purpose.

References

Benyohai, M. (2018) 'Assessment practice that is wide of the mark', *Medium* [Website], 14 August. Retrieved from: www.bit.ly/3c5wIsW

Christodoulou, D. (2017) *Making good progress? The future of assessment for learning.* Oxford: Oxford University Press.

CybSafe (2020) 'Human error to blame for 9 in 10 UK cyber data breaches in 2019', *CybSafe* [Website], 7 February. Retrieved from: www.bit.ly/2TH1LoD

Department for Education (2018) *Making data work.* London: The Stationery Office. Retrieved from: www.bit.ly/2LRJhgU

]Few, S. (2009) *Now you see it: simple visualization techniques for quantitative analysis.* El Dorado Hills, CA: Analytics Press.

Ofsted (2019) *The education inspection framework.* London: The Stationery Office. Retrieved from: www.bit.ly/2A3xBVj

Sherwood, D. (2019) '1 school exam grade in 4 is wrong. Does this matter?', *Higher Education Policy Institute* [Website], 15 January. Retrieved from: www.bit.ly/3d6mhqd

Treadaway, M. (2015) 'Why measuring pupil progress involves more than taking a straight line', *FFT Education Datalab* [Website], 5 March. Retrieved from: www.bit.ly/2K69lDC

Wiliam, D. (2014) *Principled assessment design.* London: The Schools Network.

Author bio-sketch:

Rich Davies spent six years leading on data and insight at Ark Schools. He is now helping build an outstanding alternative to university at WhiteHat. He has worked with schools in the UK and the USA and was previously a strategy consultant. He studied engineering at Oxford and both business and education at Stanford.allows us to teach better quicker.

MAKING WAVES:
A BETTER FUTURE FOR ASSESSMENT
LOIC MENZIES

Introduction

A vanguard of teachers, schools, groups of schools and countries is working towards a better future for assessment. My team and I have spent a year studying their journeys.

The innovators we studied did not always find the road easy, and the story that emerges is not one of simple, transferable solutions. However, their stories provide valuable lessons with the potential to help teachers and leaders take back control of assessment and ensure it serves pupils' needs better.

Ultimately overcoming assessment challenges involves not just finding 'the right solution' off the shelf, but also planning implementation carefully, reviewing progress regularly and adapting where necessary. This chapter sets out some of the lessons for how to do this that have emerged from our year-long study.

Innovating with responsibility

Back in 2008, I was finishing off my NQT year in North West London. After a tough trainee year, I had discovered I loved teaching; but, like many people, I was fed up with marking – or more specifically, with my school's marking policy.

I was my school's only citizenship teacher and was therefore teaching over 400 pupils a week. The school's policy was that every pupil's book had to be marked every fortnight. However, it took me around five minutes to mark each book, which meant each week I had over 15 hours of marking to do, on top of my planning and teaching.

According to TeacherTapp, that put me in the top percentile of teachers for time spent marking, but even though my experience was extreme, 1 in 20 teachers is spending over ten hours a week marking (TeacherTapp, 2017). On top of that, like many teachers, my assessment expertise was limited and I had very few strategies in my arsenal to get pupils to act on my feedback. 'Two stars and a wish' was probably the peak of my assessment prowess.

Ultimately, I was drowning trying to comply with my school's expectations, yet despite my efforts to keep up, I felt it was not helping my pupils. It felt like there were so many other better things I could do with those 15 hours a week which would have far more impact on my pupils. My cost-benefit analysis did not add up, but luckily I was in the privileged position of being confident enough of my job security to feel I could take some risks. I therefore unilaterally decided to stop marking. I was repeatedly hauled into the head's office for my actions (or lack of action) but felt I could justify my decision.

Seven years later, I co-authored *Testing the Water* (Millard et al. 2017), a report published in 2017 by Pearson and The Centre for Education and Youth (known then as LKMco). We surveyed over 1000 teachers and held focus groups all around the country with teachers, parents and young people. It revealed that my experience was far from unique; the two biggest challenges when it comes to assessment are workload and lack of assessment expertise. However, we also found that pockets of innovation were springing up, where teachers and schools were introducing new approaches with the potential to tackle these two problems. So we embarked on a new, year-long study called 'Making Waves', to understand how teachers, schools, groups of schools and countries can build a better future for assessment.

The 'Making Waves' approach

Our study focused on nine assessment innovations and took an in-depth and long-term approach by following initiatives over the course of three terms to understand how intention translates to reality.

To begin the study, we needed to find a set of assessment innovations. In keeping with our interest in teacher- and school-driven innovation, we began with a crowdsourcing campaign where we asked teachers, schools and groups of schools to share new approaches they were taking to assessment. We defined 'assessment' broadly, including everything from quick, verbal feedback during lessons through to formal examinations, and everything in between. We then worked with an advisory group to select a set of innovations to study in more detail based on four criteria:

1. **Relevance:** The proposed 'wave' is clearly focused on addressing the workload associated with assessment and/or teachers' assessment

expertise (their knowledge/understanding/skill in relation to assessment).

2. **Newness:** The 'wave' has recently been implemented (or is about to be implemented) – allowing us to study the process of implementing it and the changes that are taking place.

3. **Plausibility:** There is a plausible evidence base or rationale for how the 'wave' will lead to the intended change.

4. **Balance:** The 'wave' allows us to study a balanced basket of innovations – i.e. it is not too similar to other 'waves'.

We also sought a mix of classroom-, school-, school group- and jurisdiction-level initiatives.

Next, in order to study our wave-makers in a consistent and comparable way, we needed a clear framework. This also needed to provide a degree of flexibility given that we were looking at a range of initiatives, with some taking place at a national level whilst others were running in a single classroom.

We therefore chose to base our structure on an existing theoretical framework called the policy cycle. It was a helpful framework for us because it seeks to describe how an idea emerges, develops and is implemented. On the other hand, it is a somewhat simplistic model which has been much developed and critiqued in the field of policy studies (Howlett and Giest, 2013). As we will discover over the course of this chapter, our study in fact ended up echoing many of these criticisms and showing that they are equally pertinent when it comes to developing and implementing assessment innovations in education.

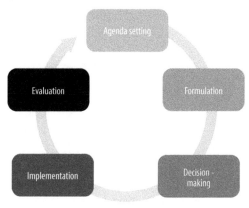

The nine wave-makers

Detailed information about each of the innovations can be found in the 'Making Waves' report, but the table below provides a brief summary.

Innovation 1: Assessment innovation team at Heathfield Community College	Staff from different departments came together in an assessment working group. They received training on assessment and designed, piloted and evaluated new initiatives (such as 'interleaving' homework or producing portfolios of exemplar work).
Innovation 2: Isaac Physics at Rickmansworth School	The school's head of physics introduced a new platform which includes thousands of questions related to different key stages and topics in physics. It generates details about pupil performance and progress.
Innovation 3: ImpactEd at Bengeworth CE Academy	ImpactEd provides schools with a data platform that allows schools to input progress data and make comparisons across pupils and across other schools. Bengeworth has worked with ImpactEd to build the collection of tools on the platform that measure non-cognitive skills such as metacognition, self-awareness and resilience and to track the impact of interventions.
Innovation 4: Shine at Eltham Hill School	Pupils in an afterschool club produce artwork in the form of memes and send these to a professional artist offsite via email through their teacher during the session. The artist gives live feedback in the form of direct comments on the work or changes to the original meme.
Innovation 5: E edi at the Academies Enterprise Trust (AET)	Eedi consists of diagnostic multiple-choice, low-stakes, formative assessment tests. Approximately 60 primary, secondary and special schools in AET – the largest MAT in England – have been using the platform. It is being used across different age groups up to year 8, and additionally with year 11.
Innovation 6: Laser conversations at the Midland Academies Trust	'Laser conversations' are an assessment practice used in all four of the secondary schools that are part of the Midland Academies Trust. They are intended to make assessment more meaningful. Rather than regularly entering pupil performance data into a system, teachers have conversations with their line managers about how pupils are progressing and what steps they are taking to support pupils who are underperforming. The process involves classroom teachers, middle leaders and senior leaders.
Innovation 7: Curriculum and assessment reform in British Columbia, Canada	The province of British Columbia is introducing wholesale curriculum and assessment reforms, shifting towards competencies and promoting practices such as self-assessment.
Innovations 8 and 9: Online assessment resource banks in New Zealand and Victoria, Australia	Both New Zealand and the state of Victoria in Australia have introduced initiatives to provide teachers with assessment resources online. They have taken different approaches and we have therefore taken a comparative approach in studying both alongside each other.

Findings
Agenda-setting

Innovation does not happen without reason, so the first stage in understanding new approaches to assessment is to pin down the reasons for moving beyond the status quo.

The four main drivers behind the innovations we studied were 'pedagogical', 'cultural', 'policy-based' and 'workforce-driven'. Whilst some of these were framed in positive ways (such as a desire to find new and better pedagogical models based on a particular educational philosophy), in most cases they were responsive, seeking to tackle perceived 'pain points'.

PEDAGOGICAL DRIVERS OF INNOVATION

All of the innovations we studied focused on improving teaching and learning rather than accountability.

In England, several innovations were natural continuations of longstanding efforts to move towards assessment for learning (Black and Wiliam, 2005). This tended to involve shortening the feedback loop between gathering assessment information and making adjustments to teaching. In some cases, these innovations tried to overcome the difficulties that can arise where teachers' limited assessment or subject expertise makes it harder to assess accurately and identify misconceptions. As one maths lead put it: '[You need to have] the subject knowledge as a teacher to think, "Why do you think that's right? What's going on in your head? What's your misconception that we need to unpick?" And that is where poor subject knowledge [from teachers] can mean that a child doesn't necessarily move forward.'

Many of these diagnostic innovations involved technology and assessment-based homework tasks. Several teachers described developing Google Forms surveys that allow them to get at-a-glance information about their class's understanding through starter activities.

Whilst these innovations were driven by positive, pedagogical considerations, they were also a response to frustration with approaches that were variously described as 'data for data's sake' and 'a lot of time wasted "weighing the pig"'.

In the countries we studied outside the UK, assessment innovation was often seen as part of a shift towards new or alternative pedagogical approaches. This can reflect ideological preferences, as well dissatisfaction with traditional assessment's almost exclusive focus on academic outcomes. For example, this was the case in British Columbia, Canada, where the new approach has involved prioritising cross-curricula goals, independent learning, self-assessment and holistic non-academic outcomes. (Will Millard, who led our fieldwork in British Columbia, writes more about our findings in the province in the next chapter.)

In England, several innovators introduced initiatives that extended what was assessed and how. But given the cultural and policy context in a system with strong, top-down accountability, they tended to do so alongside more traditional approaches. For example, Bengeworth CE Academy uses an online platform called ImpactEd which provides tools for assessing non-academic outcomes and for benchmarking progress against these. Meanwhile, Rosie Osborne, lead practitioner at Eltham Hill School, wanted to give feedback to pupils in her after-school group in a way that had real-world validity and which boosted pupils' confidence. She therefore worked with a non-teacher (a professional artist) to provide pupils with informal feedback.

CULTURAL DRIVERS OF INNOVATION

Approaches to innovation tend to reflect teachers', schools', multi-academy trusts' (MATs) or countries' cultures and values.

Several of the wave-makers we studied emphasised their belief in inclusive approaches to education and this shaped their approach to assessment. In some cases, this led them to design innovations that helped identify and respond to pupils' individual needs, whilst in others they were seeking to protect or support specific groups. This could be seen in efforts to reshape the education system to better meet indigenous groups' needs in British Columbia (Canada), Victoria (Australia), and New Zealand. In the UK, pupils with special educational needs and disabilities (SEND) were a key consideration.

Meanwhile, Heathfield Community College wanted to reflect its intended professional culture when reforming its assessment practices. They therefore invited staff to volunteer for an 'assessment innovation team' in which teachers from different subject groups researched and developed new approaches to assessment tailored to their discipline and pedagogy. Departments then trialled and compared practice. This contrasts with a common perception that rigid assessment systems can act as tools of compliance that undermine professional autonomy. Similarly, teachers' retaining the freedom to select questions themselves helps preserve their autonomy, and this is seen as one of the advantages of assessment banks like those used in AET's schools and in New Zealand.

Some contexts seem to provide particularly fertile ground for innovation. In these settings, there was said to be an overall appetite for innovation and new ways of doing things. This could be seen in some schools which described themselves as particularly engaged in research, or in British Columbia where policymakers referred to the province's desire to be at the cutting edge of global educational innovation and reform.

POLICY-LEVEL DRIVERS OF INNOVATION

National shifts in policy can drive innovation at school level. The assessment innovation team at Heathfield Community College was partly set up in response to the government's decision to move to 'assessment without levels', whilst the biology department there developed its approach partly in response to a perceived increase in curriculum rigour. Meanwhile, Bengeworth CE Academy's priorities were influenced by changes in the Ofsted framework, SEND code of practice and 'national agenda'.

Policy drivers are also linked to school funding, which can push schools to pursue innovations that promise enhanced value for money.

WORKFORCE DRIVERS OF INNOVATION

In *Testing the Water*, we found that assessment is often linked to excessive teacher workload. We were therefore particularly interested in innovations that responded to the urgent need to reduce workload.

Beyond concerns about workload in absolute terms, we found that innovators sometimes distinguished between 'worthwhile' and 'less worthwhile' workload, arguing that what mattered was ensuring teachers spent less time on unproductive or meaningless activities. This sentiment was echoed by our advisory group. A requirement not to add to workload was also a key design principle that sat behind most innovations.

Some schools and MATs selected their approach in response to struggles in securing the workforce they needed, particularly in subjects like maths and physics that are plagued by teacher shortages.

Formulation and decision-making

Once innovators spot an issue with assessment, they formulate their response and decide on a solution. A simple, rational choice-based version of the policy cycle sees decision-making as a process of comparing different options, weighing them up and selecting the best one. However, in the field of policy studies, it is argued that decision-making is more often incremental or based on 'satisficing' (where rather than maximising benefits over costs, a solution is selected so long as it seems to minimally satisfy the criteria set by decision-makers) (Howlett and Giest, 2013). Meanwhile, others argue that 'decision-making is affected by the number of agents involved in a decision, their organisational set, how well a problem is defined, the information available on the problem, its causes and consequences and the amount of time available to decision-makers to consider possible contingencies and their present and anticipated consequences' (pp. 20–21). We found features of all of these factors in the genesis of the innovations we studied. It also seemed that the processes of formulation and decision-making were rarely discrete, so whilst it would be unfair to describe the decisions we studied as 'non-rational', they were rarely based on dispassionate optimisation.

A range of individuals are involved in shaping and making decisions about assessment innovations, and they all have differing priorities and lenses through which they look at issues. Decisions were sometimes prompted by alignment between complementary political agendas and at other times arose when the same initiative ticked boxes for individuals with slightly different pedagogical agendas such as parental engagement, raising attainment, curriculum reform, and assessment rigour.

Once a possible answer to a pain point had been found, alternatives were rarely considered and weighed up. Innovators tended to proceed stepwise from one initiative to another with initiatives frequently responding to a previous approach, taking it to the next level, or rejecting and replacing it. Typical reasons for previous failures were excessive cost, labour-intensive approaches that provided limited valuable information, and approaches that tried but failed to serve multiple competing functions (such as predicting performance alongside guiding teaching and intervention).

The 'bounded rationality' that drove the decisions we studied is understandable. Schools and teachers are time poor and, where time is a constraint, it may be more efficient to proceed more iteratively. On the other hand, this runs the risk of wasting time when the chosen option does not work as well as it could.

A number of approaches can minimise this risk. Innovators often identified an approach that was already working well and extended it, or applied it in different contexts or cases. Examples of this include building an assessment innovation team based on a school's existing successful use of innovation teams focused on other themes, or identifying a practice within one school in a MAT and implementing it across different settings, as the Midland Academies Trust did.

Another MAT built some degree of stress-testing into its decision-making through what it called 'thoughtful disagreement':

> We thrashed it out with the team. We always encourage absolute open debate and disagreement. We call it thoughtful disagreement. … We ask people to play devil's advocate. … It's not about the loudest voice at winning the arguments; it's about the most compelling reasoning and logic.

Research and learning from others also played a role in directing innovators to certain solutions, but this was not based on extensive searches through a broad range of literature. Instead, certain high-profile researchers like Daisy Christodoulou, Dylan Wiliam and Becky Allen were repeatedly mentioned, while other innovators drew ideas from their close peers.

Context shapes and constrains options in many ways, making some innovations opportunistic or 'bounding' the options that can be rationally selected. For example, the status quo shaped online assessment platforms in Victoria, Australia, and in New Zealand, due to factors such as who owned data, platforms and tools. Meanwhile in British Columbia, decisions were said to be limited by the Overton window – the range of policies and educational ideas deemed acceptable at any one time.

Ultimately, the decisions we studied were made by individuals and groups of individuals, and this shaped the outcome. At Heathfield Community College, the head of geography's approach was influenced by the fact that they were also the school research lead, while the head of photography's background as a sports coach shaped their approach. This means that those with power – in terms of both their degree of autonomy and their background and beliefs – shape decisions.

Implementation

Implementing an innovation involves taking an idea, putting it into practice and (in most cases) disseminating or rolling it out. Approaches to doing this vary depending on how an initiative is taken beyond the initiator, how much flexibility and adaptation there is, and the role of external partners.

DISSEMINATION MECHANISMS

Most approaches to dissemination can be characterised as a form of 'cascading'. In other words, they start with an initial node – which might be an individual, group or organisation – and are then widened out from there. Selecting and deploying an approach to cascading is therefore a critical element of implementation.

Both of the MATs we studied had spread an approach out from a central team to their schools. In the larger MAT, the central team disseminated their new approach through conferences, while in the smaller MAT, dissemination at times worked in both directions, with practices being taken from an individual school to the MAT and then out to the wider network. The context of being a small MAT made this easier and much of the dissemination happened informally, although the MAT established certain guidelines and requirements.

As we will see below, the degree of flexibility given to schools when disseminating has important implications, and in both cases the MATs have since provided further guidance and direction on how the initiatives should be implemented, or they plan to do so provide in the future.

Where innovations were introduced at school level, cascading happened between departments. At the jurisdiction level, cascading took place from national, provincial or state ministries to districts, and in turn to schools. Flexibility was built into British Columbia's model with districts' approaches differing in a number of ways, again raising important questions regarding flexibility versus rigidity.

FLEXIBILITY AND RIGIDITY

Innovators did not tend to take their idea and roll it out as a finished product, or expect it to be implemented with total fidelity to the original plan. In some cases, flexibility was built in through piloting. For example, Bengeworth CE Academy trialled ImpactEd with a small number of academic and non-academic interventions before adopting it more fully. In other cases, flexibility involved a more organic process of evolution and adaptation, with challenges identified throughout and modifications made in response. While this approach may be well suited to developing a new approach, it can make it harder to test the effectiveness of an approach once the idea matures. Furthermore, a flexible approach can mean that innovations stray from their original intentions and innovators therefore need to identify the golden core of their approach so they can establish non-negotiables as it evolves.

EXTERNAL PARTNERSHIPS

Innovators rarely work on their own. Even individual teachers implementing small-scale initiatives drew on expertise and resources from beyond the school, whether a professional artist in the case of Eltham Hill or an established technological product combined with a network of other teachers at Rickmansworth.

In some cases, external partners provided a tool or platform, whereas in others they provided expertise and training, or a combination of both.

AET and Bengeworth CE Academy both emphasised the importance of a close relationship with their external provider, since this allowed them to co-develop the platforms, adapting and tailoring them to their teachers' and pupils' needs. Importantly, the close partnership meant the provider could provide training and respond quickly to any problems. Meanwhile, Heathfield Community College sourced expertise from a university and – much like the training provided by the New Zealand Council for Educational Research (NZCER) and the Victorian Curriculum and Assessment Authority (VCAA) – this empowered teachers by giving them the assessment expertise they needed in order to become assessment innovators.

FACILITATING FACTORS AND BARRIERS TO SUCCESS

As explored above, effective dissemination, getting the right balance between flexibility and standardisation, relationships with external providers and the availability of training can all affect how successfully an innovation is implemented. Beyond these, a number of practical considerations can contribute to or detract from successful implementation, as can the degree of alignment between stakeholders.

Practicalities

We saw our wave-makers grapple with a number of practical issues such as homework completion rates and access to technology.

Ultimately, over the course of our study it became clear that several of the initiatives we were tracking were highly vulnerable to changes in resourcing. Innovation can be expensive and success depends on adequate resources – not just in terms of funding but also training and freeing up teachers' time. It is for this reason that AET now plans to award a teaching and learning responsibility (TLR) payment for Eedi champions, and why the Midland Academies Trust is keen to find time-savings in other areas (such as 'tick and flick' marking) to free up time for one-to-one conversations about pupil achievement.

Alignment

Securing and maintaining backing from a coalition of supporters makes it easier to ensure an innovation remains a priority for all those involved. Developing and making a strong case for an innovation is therefore an important part of implementation.

As we saw earlier, innovations often gain traction when 'the stars align' and several different agendas come together. Innovators therefore found that securing buy-in from leaders at different levels – as well as from parents and pupils – helped oil the wheels of implementation. In contrast, implementation often suffered when one group struggled to understand the innovation or where sceptics could not be persuaded of its value.

In some cases, innovators secured and maintained support by demonstrating impact; Rosie Osborne (lead practitioner at Eltham Hill School) reported that senior leaders trusted her to run her innovation because they could see that students were more engaged in their learning thanks to their after-school projects. She created the conditions for this recognition by maintaining an open-door policy that allowed senior leaders to drop into sessions and see her work in action. Similarly, results from a mini control-group trial are making it easier for the head of biology at Heathfield Community College to persuade others of her approach. Her early decisions about evaluation have therefore contributed to successful implementation. Meanwhile at Bengeworth CE Academy, the leadership team considered discontinuing their use of ImpactEd, but eventually backed deeper and broader implementation because Rachel Seneque (the head of inclusion) was able to show long-term potential for financial savings.

Evaluation

We did not generally find a tight link between the impact innovators originally intended to have and the indicators of success that they referred to when describing their approaches to evaluation. Notions of success included the following:

- improved academic results and progression
- pupil and parental engagement
- uptake and usage of a platform or tool
- reduced workload or time savings
- improved use of evidence
- changes in pedagogy – in particular, better use of assessment information

- improved non-cognitive skills
- shifts in mindsets and educational approach
- inclusion
- better relationships between teachers and pupils

Very few wave-makers evaluated their initiatives formally and it could be argued that this means initiatives will not lead to their intended changes, or that success will go unnoticed. On the other hand, many initiatives were at an early stage where processes and approaches were still being refined. Many argued that this made rapid and flexible adaptation a greater priority than a formal evaluation. Innovators were also fearful of creating rigidity prematurely.

Gathering feedback was therefore considered a more pressing priority and many innovators favoured informal assessments of whether pupil work and engagement were improving. Others decided that usage of a tool was a good proxy for whether an initiative was effective. For example, in New Zealand, one interviewee argued that the ARBs did not need to be evaluated because their popularity was sufficient evidence of success. Unfortunately, however, this assumes that all popular initiatives are effective.

On the other hand, in some cases innovators recognised that in order to gauge success they needed to triangulate between different sources of information. At AET these included a usage tracker, book scrutiny by regional curriculum leads, and upward cascading of feedback from schools' maths leads via regional leads all the way up to the central team through the individuals responsible for school engagement.

Whilst there is clearly a compromise needed between flexibility and rigorous methods for gauging efficacy, Heathfield's approach may offer a model that balances these two competing priorities since it combines small-scale innovation at departmental level with planned but flexible evaluation.

Conclusion

Having spent the last year exploring assessment innovations, I cannot help looking back and reflecting on my time in teaching and my own marking rebellion. In retrospect, I am still glad I did not sacrifice all those hours marking books, and I am glad that I challenged my school's policies. However, with the benefit of hindsight and increased engagement with research, what I now realise is the importance of innovating with responsibility. Like many innovators, I (and my pupils) might have benefited from a slightly more thoughtful and evidence-based formulation and decision-making phase, rather than picking the first satisficing option that I came across. I could also have considered implementation and evaluation more, thinking through how to bring others on board, and making my case while reviewing my decision's impact more carefully, rather than simply enduring the inevitable summonses to the head's office.

This chapter, and the full 'Making Waves' study, are intended to support teachers, schools and countries to innovate in assessment with responsibility. They are designed to help teachers recognise the pain points they want to address, and to find new ideas to formulate their own innovations. I hope they will also provide some guidance on how to plan for effective implementation. An innovation's impact is often determined as much by its implementation as it is by the quality of the idea itself.

References

Black, P. and Wiliam, D. (2005) *Inside the black box: raising standards through classroom assessment.* London: Granada Learning.

Howlett, M. and Giest, S. (2013) 'The policy-making process' in Araral, E., Fritzen, S., Howlett, M., Ramesh, M. and Wu, X. (eds) *Routledge handbook of public policy.* London: Routledge.

Millard, W., Small, I. and Menzies, L. (2017) *Testing the water: how assessment can underpin, not undermine, great teaching.* London: Pearson/LKMco. Retrieved from: www.bit.ly/3cjI10B

TeacherTapp (2017) 'Marking like no-one is watching', *TeacherTapp* [Blog], 15 November. Retrieved from: www.bit.ly/2LukjnJ

Author bio-sketch:

Loic Menzies is chief executive of The Centre for Education and Youth. He has previously worked as a teacher, youth worker and tutor for Canterbury Christ Church's Faculty of Education. He has authored numerous reports and works with policy makers and practitioners to communicate the implications of research.

MAKING CURRICULUM AND ASSESSMENT FIT FOR THE 21ST CENTURY?

COMPARING REFORMS IN BRITISH COLUMBIA AND ENGLAND

WILL MILLARD

There is nothing quite like seeing an education system with your own eyes to get a sense of how it works. In 2010, when the coalition government took power, I was teaching English at a secondary school in North West London. I clearly remember how Michael Gove's reforms immediately began to reshape the school's behaviour. I moved into policy research in 2012 and I spent considerable time over the next few years keeping up with the ongoing reforms to curriculum and assessment, a process that involved lots of reading as well as many hours of conversation with teachers and school leaders.

In 2019, I gained a similar overview of reforms to curriculum and assessment underway in British Columbia (BC), the vast province on Canada's west coast. I made three trips there throughout the year for The Centre for Education and Youth (CfEY) and Pearson's 'Making Waves' research (Menzies, 2018), examining how different assessment innovations have impacted upon teachers' workload and confidence. During these trips, I met and spoke with teachers, policymakers, academics, politicians, parents and young people to understand why BC's reforms were introduced, and how they are taking shape. (The previous chapter – written by CfEY's chief executive, Loic Menzies – talks more about 'Making Waves' and its findings.)

By coincidence, England and BC have both undergone extensive processes of curriculum and assessment reform since the early 2010s. While it was not deliberate on my part, I am a witness to the development of both systems, and this chapter sets out some of my thoughts about these respective journeys.

I begin by providing a brief and primarily descriptive overview of some of the key changes that have been underway in each system (which is intended to provide context for readers, wherever in the world they are reading this book), before offering some analysis based on my research to highlight some intriguing similarities and differences between England's and BC's experiences of reform, as well as some of the challenges both systems have faced.

What is happening?
Reforming curriculum and assessment in British Columbia

Sweeping reforms to curriculum and assessment are underway in the Western-Canadian province of British Columbia (BC). The Ministry of Education launched the new curriculum for kindergarten to grade 9 in 2015/16, and grades 10 to 12 in 2017/18.[8] This has been accompanied by simultaneous shifts in assessment. It is the first time in BC's recent history that such a comprehensive set of curriculum and assessment reforms have been implemented. The curriculum and assessment system is now being implemented in schools and districts across the province.

The revised curriculum is structured around:

- 'Content' ('Know'), outlining the subject-specific content at each grade level
- 'Curricular Competencies' ('Do'), outlining competencies specific to different areas of learning (such as 'questioning and predicting' in science). These link to core competencies and can stretch across multiple grade levels.
- 'Big Ideas' ('Understand'), highlighting the key principles and concepts covered during each grade. For example, that 'DNA is the basis for the diversity of living things' in grade 10 biology

(Government of British Columbia, 2020a)

Literacy and numeracy are 'applied in all areas of learning', although English and maths are also included as discrete subjects.

Three 'Core Competencies' underpin the curriculum as a whole. These represent 'intellectual, personal, and social and emotional proficiencies that

---

8.   The grade structure in British Columbia is roughly equivalent to year groupings in England. Kindergarten caters for children aged 5, grade 9 for pupils aged 13 and 14, and grade 12 for pupils aged 17 and 18.

all students need in order to engage in deep, lifelong learning' (Government of British Columbia, 2020b). Each Core Competency contains sub-competencies. The Core Competencies and related sub-competencies are:

1. 'Communication', comprising 'Communicating' and 'Collaborating'
2. 'Thinking', comprising 'Creative Thinking' and 'Critical and Reflective Thinking'
3. 'Personal and Social', comprising 'Personal Awareness and Responsibility', 'Positive Personal and Cultural Identity' and 'Social Awareness and Responsibility'

The Core Competencies provide the overarching outcomes that learning across the curriculum seeks to support. The following graphics, taken from the BC Ministry of Education's website, show how the curriculum is visualised (Government of British Columbia, 2020c):

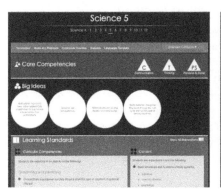 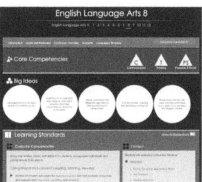

Alongside the new curriculum, BC has introduced far-reaching changes in assessment. The new system is characterised by:

- Teacher assessment of the Curricular Competencies (with the competencies spanning grade levels in different areas of learning)
- The piloting of a proficiency scale for reporting pupils' achievements in each area of learning at each grade ('emerging', 'developing', 'proficient' and 'extending')
- Students self-assessing (and reporting) against the Core Competencies at least once a year throughout their education
- Numeracy and literacy assessments replacing exams in grades 10 and 12. Students must take these assessments in order to graduate,

although they do not need to pass them. Students sit fewer assessments (having previously taken assessments in a wider range of subjects), and part of the assessment involves a self-reflection activity.

- Revised formats for foundational skills assessments in grades 4 and 7, a set of paper and online reading, writing, and numeracy assessments administered each year. These are intended to provide a snapshot of system-level performance. Parents and teachers can opt children out of these assessments.

(Government of British Columbia, 2020d)

In terms of how the curriculum is presented, and how pupils' achievements are assessed and reported (particularly in terms of moving emphasis away from summative judgements towards formative feedback and self-assessment), the new arrangements represent a significant shift from the previous system.

Reforming curriculum and assessment in England

Since the coalition government took power in 2010, the school system in England has undergone extensive reform, including to curriculum and assessment. Following several years of design and consultation, the new curriculum was introduced and taught in schools from September 2014. Key features of this revised curriculum include:

- An emphasis on English, maths and science across key stages 1 to 4, but particularly at primary school (key stages 1 and 2), including the promotion and testing of synthetic phonics and spelling, punctuation and grammar
- Comparatively less content specified in other areas of the curriculum
- The introduction of new subjects, such as computing
- More explicit, age-related expectations, outlining what pupils should learn and when (exemplified in the graphics below, taken from the KS1 maths programme of study)

(Department for Education, 2014; Roberts, 2019)

The following graphics show how this content is presented:

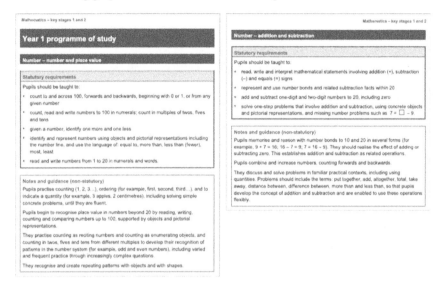

The national curriculum sets out teachers' obligations to make learning inclusive and to build linguistic and mathematics fluency in 'every relevant subject' (Department for Education, 2014).

Importantly, academies (another flagship coalition government education reform) are not required to teach the national curriculum. However, SATs and GCSEs (the assessments at the end of primary and secondary schooling, respectively) and school accountability measures mean most academies base their curricula around the national curriculum.

Alongside curriculum reform, far-reaching changes have been made to assessment. A period of design and consultation led up to the teaching of new GCSEs and A levels from September 2015, with additional new exam content introduced in 2016 and 2017. Key changes in the approaches to assessment included a shift towards 'linear' courses with exams at the end (as opposed to throughout), and a concurrent reduction in coursework. A new 9 to 1 grading system replaced letter grades at GCSE, and A level and AS levels were decoupled, meaning AS levels no longer contributed towards A level results (Long, 2017).

At key stages 1 and 2, levels (the bedrock of assessment for over a decade) were removed and replaced with a proficiency scale indicating whether pupils are 'emerging', 'expected' or 'exceeding' in relation to the curriculum (Poet et al., 2018; Roberts, 2020).

Why is this happening?
Three justifications for reform

In both systems, the reforms were comprehensive, involving root-and-branch changes to curriculum and assessment. Something that struck me during my visits to BC was how similar some of the justifications for the reforms were to those given in England, even though – as I will go on to explore – opinions on how to improve standards were diametrically opposite. In both places, three main justifications have been given:

1. THE NEED TO MODERNISE AND KEEP PACE

Both systems introduced far-reaching reforms to ensure their education systems would modernise and 'keep pace'. British Columbia is perceived to have a highly effective education system and has been described as an educational 'superpower' (Coughlan, 2017). However, anxious not to rest on their laurels, policymakers and educationalists in BC stressed the need for the system to modernise and adapt to the changing world. The Ministry's website explains that the curriculum was previously 'modelled on the very different circumstances of an earlier century', and that technology has changed what and how students learn:

> Today we live in a state of constant change. It is a technology-rich world, where communication is instant and information is immediately accessible. ... British Columbia's curriculum is being modernized to respond to this demanding world. (Government of British Columbia, 2020e)

Likewise, in England, 'standing still' was not good enough, and a political justification for reforming education was to improve the country's performance in international league tables. In contrast with British Columbia, in 2010 England was a mid-ranking jurisdiction in international assessments, and policymakers were keen to catch up with the top performers (at the time, Finland and South Korea):

> What really matters is how we're doing compared with our international competitors. That is what will define our economic growth and our country's future. The truth is, at the moment we are standing still while others race past. (Department for Education, 2010)

Politicians and policymakers characterised their own systems as sclerotic in order to provide impetus for change. In a nutshell, and as one BC district assistant superintendent[9] put it, 'the world is changing and education needs to change'.

2. THE NEED TO IMPROVE TEACHING AND LEARNING

In both jurisdictions, reforms were justified on the basis of needing to improve the quality and consistency of teaching and learning. In BC, I spoke to politicians, policymakers at the Ministry of Education, academics and educators including superintendents and teachers who felt pedagogy needed to evolve in order to remain effective and relevant. Generally, interviewees felt that while many teachers already practise the 'right' sorts of pedagogy, the curriculum and assessment reforms would help raise the bar across the system as a whole:

> I'm not going to set up educational systems for dinosaurs when mammals are thriving. They're going to be extinct soon enough. And there's already pressure, a fair amount of pressure on them, to either leave, or bring up the standard.

Dr Kris Magnusson, dean of education, Simon Fraser University

In England, a key justification by government for its education reforms (including reforms to curriculum and assessment) was the need to improve the quality of teaching and learning (Department for Education, 2010).

I will look later at the sorts of classroom practice endorsed by each set of curriculum and assessment reforms.

3. THE NEED TO IMPROVE OUTCOMES FOR DISADVANTAGED COMMUNITIES

Another similarity in both jurisdictions has been the need to better support communities facing disadvantage and experiencing worse educational outcomes.

Nationwide in Canada, there has been an extensive process of truth and reconciliation, seeking to acknowledge and take steps towards addressing the damage inflicted on indigenous communities by settlers. This has been felt acutely in BC because of the province's relatively high indigenous population, and also because of the worse educational outcomes people from these communities tend to experience (graduation rates are lower, for example).

---

9.   A superintendent and their team are responsible for standards and budgets in a
     school district

This has therefore been a major focus of the reforms, and indigenous – or 'First Nations' – representatives played a central role in the formulation of the revised curriculum and approaches to assessment. For example, the First Nations Education Steering Committee (FNESC) was given seats on each of the Ministry's curriculum committees. As one senior policymaker within the Ministry put it, 'we don't do anything without the involvement of our indigenous educator colleagues'.

Similarly in England, the achievement of pupils from poorer backgrounds lay 'at the heart' of the reform programme, supported by the introduction of the pupil premium, additional funding that followed 'poorer children directly to the school they attend' (Department for Education, 2010). While there has been substantial disagreement since then about the most effective ways of achieving greater equity for disadvantaged pupils, this has undeniably been a central justification for many of the government's reforms in education. It is also questionable whether these communities have been actively involved in the way that they were in BC.

Differences of opinion regarding how to improve standards

Despite these similarities in terms of underlying justification, there are significant differences in how reform has been approached in England and BC:

'PROGRESSIVE' VERSUS 'TRADITIONAL' MODELS OF EDUCATION
'Progressivism' in BC

Reforms in BC have taken an unashamedly 'progressive' bent. Personalised learning is a key tenet of the revised curriculum and also something assessment seeks to promote. The curriculum should be implemented through 'flexible learning environments' spanning school, home and other settings, deploying technology, and rooted in inquiry-and question-based approaches to learning (Government of British Columbia, 2020d).

Despite BC's world-class performance in international assessments such as PISA, policymakers and educators felt pupils' excellent subject knowledge was not matched by their personal and social development, nor their ability to communicate. As a member of the Ministry's curriculum design team put it, the curriculum 'is about human development. ... Curriculum? ... That's the vehicle, not the end destination.' One university professor involved in designing the curriculum explained that it was written to develop pupils' sense of social responsibility and ability to connect with others.

The ideas and approaches set out under the revised BC curriculum were first proposed in the 1988 Sullivan report, written as a response to the 'unprecedented challenges' posed by shifting economic and technological trends (Sullivan, 1988). More extensive plans within the Ministry to embed the Sullivan report's recommendations were abandoned in the 1990s due to concern among parents and teachers about a potential drop in academic standards (Kilian, 2011; Sanford and Hopper, 2019). However, educators and policymakers still cite the Sullivan report as 'foundational' in shaping their thinking about education, with its ideas being 'dusted off' as the new reforms began to take shape.

Some describe BC as the 'Left Coast', suggesting progressive educational views exist against a backdrop of progressive, left-leaning social and political norms. Indeed, many of the key architects of the curriculum share a broadly progressive educational outlook. That is to say that they stress the important of individualised and student-led learning that emphasises skills and competencies over and above pure 'knowledge' and more didactic pedagogic styles. Politicians and senior policymakers cite the likes of high-profile progressive educationalists such as John Abbott (author of Overschooled But Undereducated') and Ken Robinson as influences on their thinking:

> The kind of Ken Robinson approach to revitalising education I think had significant currency in British Columbia for probably a couple of decades.

George Abbott, former Minister of Education

'Traditionalism' in England

In England, a rather different set of educational preferences were taking hold (certainly among politicians) during the early 2010s, prizing a focus on knowledge and teacher-led styles of pedagogy. This re-orientation was justified by its advocates as necessary in undoing many years of damage inflicted by 'progressive' educational approaches, and ministers shaping England's educational policies have made little secret of their views on teaching and learning, specifying a preference for more 'traditional' approaches (Gibb, 2017).

The reforms focused on 'rigour'. For example, the emphasis placed on English, maths and science throughout the curriculum (particularly at primary) would – it was argued – improve the quality of teaching and learning throughout schooling. Furthermore, reforms to assessment would provide an antidote to exam boards' 'race to the bottom' in which competing exam boards were accused of attempting to make their assessments easier to gain 'market share' by making their 'products' more appealing to schools that were eager to boost their results (Cook, 2011).

It is striking that while BC doubled down on its progressive preferences, in England reforms meant changing direction. Modernising the system in England involved (some would say) turning back the clock. Unlike in BC, where the Liberal Party had been in power for a decade by the time it initiated the reforms and was keen to embed its legacy, in England the new coalition government elected in 2010 was keen to make its mark.

STUDENT- AND TEACHER-ASSESSMENT VERSUS 'PEN AND PAPER' EXAMS
Student- and teacher-led assessment in BC
In BC, assessment has been reconfigured in order to encourage a far wider array of assessment methods beyond paper-and-pen tests. Assessments reforms were intended to improve the quality of assessment by:

- Drawing students into the reporting process so that they take greater ownership over their learning
- Prioritising formative assessment over summative tests
- Raising students' awareness of how they learn, as well as what they learn
- Giving students a greater role in their own learning, ensuring they are not spoon fed
- Promoting the use of positive language and 'strength-based' assessment that describes what students can do, rather than grades
- Helping students to self- and peer-assess
- Re-positioning teachers as facilitators of learning, rather than 'lecturers'
- Supporting a wider range of assessment methods (for example, shifting away from a reliance on quizzes and tests towards using observation, interviews, dialogue, e-portfolios, and so on)

The Ministry's Curriculum and Assessment Framework Advisory Group was one of the first advisory groups convened to begin designing the curriculum. One of its members explained:

We have a long history of student self-assessment in this province. … We did that work extensively in the late '90s and early 2000s and all through the 2000s, and so formative assessment and student self-assessment was something we'd been working on extensively. So the idea of self-assessment for the core competencies built on a practice that we were familiar with.

Dr Leyton Schnellert, associate professor, Faculty of Education, University of British Columbia

Furthermore, these approaches to assessment, and students' self-assessment in particular, solved a perceived conundrum:

We kept coming back to the fact that the only person in the process who had enough knowledge of all the various pieces to summarise and report on them was the student.

Sharon Jeroski, former advisor to Ministry of Education

Likewise, over time it was hoped that as the reforms embedded, it would reduce teachers', parents' and students' reliance on summative grades and percentages. There were two key motivations for this. The first was the hope that it would instil a greater focus on 'next steps' and improve students' learning experiences. The second was that it would be fairer, offering a more inclusive way of assessing students – particularly those at risk of marginalisation.

'Paper-and-pen' assessment in England

The direction of travel in England has been very different. Post-2010 reforms have emphasised the importance of paper-and-pen testing at the end of primary, secondary and post-16 schooling. For example, a higher proportion of both GCSE and A level assessments are conducted at the end of the courses of study, and in 'sit down' exams.

Paradoxically, the reasons for this are – in some ways – the same as those given in BC. Namely, to improve the quality of assessment and simultaneously make assessment fairer.

On the first point, the quality of an assessment is inextricably linked to its function or purpose. It is therefore not the case *a priori* that tests and exams taken in an exam hall at the end of courses of study are better quality. However, some argue that exams *are* a good way to conduct an assessment if its function is to provide a reliable indication of what most pupils in a particular cohort know about a subject at a given point in time (Christodoulou, 2017).

Furthermore, advocates claim that exams are fairer than assessments that rely on teacher observation. These are issues explored in CfEY and Pearson's 2017 report, *Testing the Water* (Millard et al., 2017). While teacher assessment is a vitally important part of the learning process, teachers are subject to the same biases as everyone else, and can unfairly (if unconsciously) discriminate against pupils on the basis of characteristics such as gender, ethnicity or even BMI (Burgess and Greaves, 2013).

This issue came to a head in England during a dispute about the assessment of speaking and listening. This teacher assessment had been part of the English GCSE, but was scrapped by Ofqual in 2013 because of evidence teachers were inflating pupils' performance (Stacey, 2013).

CONSENSUS BUILDING VERSUS BULLDOZERS
Building bridges in BC
The reforms in BC provided a politically expedient opportunity to begin mending woeful relations between the Ministry and BC's only teachers' union, the BCTF (British Columbia Teachers' Federation). The two had been embroiled in a savage legal dispute for years. Consequently, Minister George Abbott's first call as minister was to the then BCTF president, Susan Lambert:

> [I said], 'Hey, this may surprise you, but I wanted to make my first phone call as a minister to you. It's no secret that our government has had a poor relationship with you for a long time. I'd like to see if we can change that.'

George Abbott, former Minister of Education

While the reforms provided an opportunity to build bridges, the Ministry also wanted the BCTF's input to legitimise the reforms and ensure teachers found them palatable. One senior policymaker at the Ministry said the aim was to introduce reforms so popular that teachers 'would strike' if the reforms were reversed.

This commitment to consultation continued throughout the curriculum and assessment design phases. The Ministry established numerous committees involving stakeholders from right across the education system and beyond, including teachers (with the BCTF nominating representatives for every committee), school leaders and administrators, academics, and employers. One senior Ministry official said the process was almost more important than the output; what mattered was including a wide range of people.[10]

Burning bridges in England

In England, however, the approach was less conciliatory. One of the more extreme examples of this was the then Education Secretary's attack on 'the Blob', whom he described as '[a] tiny minority of teachers who ... have enlisted as Enemies Of Promise. They are the ultra-militants in the unions who are threatening strikes' (Gove, 2013).

This was the backdrop against which root-and-branch reforms to curriculum and assessment were taking place. My intention here is not to comment on the content of the revised curriculum, but rather to highlight a distinct difference in rhetoric and design process.

The process of redesigning curriculum and assessment *did* involve extensive consultation, but nonetheless teachers and unions (among others) were often at loggerheads with the Department for Education (or perhaps, more specifically, its ministers). One member of the expert panel for the national curriculum review described its proposals as 'fatally flawed'. The process for selecting and reporting evidence was described as 'selective' and 'tendentious', and the National Union of Teachers (now the National Education Union) said the revised curriculum would 'stultify the learning process' (Roberts, 2019).

Challenges in implementation

Designing policy is one thing; implementing it quite another. In both countries, getting the new systems up and running has proven challenging, which is unsurprising considering the wide scope of the reforms and the fact that the previous approaches had been in place for many years. The challenges associated with England's reforms have been well documented (Poet et al., 2018). However, I think there are three similarities about the challenges faced in England and BC:

1. SUPPORT FOR TEACHERS

Teachers in both systems have complained about a lack of support during periods of reform, and in particular a lack of guidance. Teachers in England felt this particularly acutely when levels were removed. Levels had been the

---

10.   In practice, the inclusiveness of the process was something people had mixed views on. This is explored in more depth in CfEY's report *Making Waves.*

bedrock of the assessment system across key stages 1 to 3, and their removal, without guidance on how to replace them, left many schools floundering. Some onlookers have highlighted the risk (and sometimes reality) of teachers duplicating effort and reinventing the wheel, replacing levels with approaches to assessment that are levels in all but name (Fordham, 2014).

Likewise in BC, many teachers felt they needed greater support to understand the reforms' content and how best to respond (British Columbia Teachers' Federation, 2017). Again this has led to a situation wherein teachers have duplicated effort, and one teacher said he felt the lack of resources available to help teachers (and especially new teachers) implement the changes presents a real challenge:

> There's very little resources and very little training. ... Maybe in theory it is centralised, but it's not. ... I've had to create my stuff from scratch.

Middle school teacher

In BC, teachers have relied upon their school and/or district for support and guidance, meaning some feel much better supported than others. This is analogous with teachers in England feeling better or worse supported depending on the speed and clarity with which their school, local authority or multi-academy trust responded to the reforms.

2. PARENTAL UNDERSTANDING AND BUY-IN

In both systems, parents have found it tricky to understand the new assessment systems and it has been hard for schools to communicate pupils' achievements. In England, parents of primary school children have had to grapple with shifting from levels to descriptors about whether their children are 'emerging', 'meeting' or 'exceeding' expectations; at secondary, they are adjusting to numbered grades at GCSE.

In BC, parents are acclimatising to new assessment processes (for example, the use of online portfolios to communicate pupils' achievements and progress over time). They are also adjusting to the switch away from largely summative reporting, centred on letter grades and percentages, to other forms of feedback including pupils' self-assessments and the adoption of a proficiency scale (which uses very similar language to the descriptors in use at primary in England). While many teachers and parents are in favour of this switch, others have found it problematic, especially where families have relied historically on summative judgements. In some districts, parents' scepticism has been compounded by a lack of consistency in reporting under the new frameworks; some teachers provide narrative feedback, and others continue to use grades and percentages. One student told us her parents 'hate' the new proficiency-scale-based system because they do not understand it.

3. JOINING THE DOTS BETWEEN DIFFERENT PARTS OF THE EDUCATION SYSTEM

Both systems have struggled to align needs and preferences across the education system. In BC, this was a particular concern among secondary school students and teachers, concerned about how universities will interpret and use the new assessments when making decisions about admissions. Some pupils also felt this could lead to their prospects of university entrance being at the mercy of individual teachers' judgements:

> The thing that I was really concerned [about was that] they (the government) took off the provincial assessments and they just put the numeracy and the English assessments aside. We don't know if the universities are looking at that. Now we're just solely based on the teachers' marks on us.

Secondary school student, British Columbia

We spoke to universities in BC (including staff at Simon Fraser University, University of British Columbia, and University of Victoria) who said they were adjusting their admissions procedures and that, in some cases, they felt the new assessment system had advantages, providing a more holistic view of students' achievements and potential. However, we also heard that some were introducing new entrance exams in order to benchmark and make judgements about applicants.

In England, reforms to primary assessment caused challenges for primary and secondary settings alike, with secondaries struggling (at least initially) to use SATs results to understand pupils' prior academic achievement. Outside education, understanding of the new GCSE system is low (particularly among employers), but improving (Ofqual, 2016; 2017).

Conclusion

It is coincidence that I have witnessed first hand some of the changes underway in schools in England and BC, and I was fortunate and privileged to meet such a wide array of thoughtful people working in these systems. The two systems have sought to reform their approaches to curriculum and assessment in such utterly different ways, yet for such similar underlying reasons. With their respective rankings in international league tables providing some of the motivation for reform, perhaps over time we will be able to judge for ourselves which approach has proven more successful.

References

British Columbia Teachers' Federation (2017) *2017 BCTF curriculum change and implementation survey.* Retrieved from: www.bit.ly/2XQZS9R

Burgess, S. and Greaves, E. (2013) 'Test scores, subjective assessment and stereotyping of ethnic minorities', *Journal of Labor Economics* 31 (3) pp. 535–576.

Christodoulou, D. (2017) *Making good progress?: The future of assessment for learning.* Oxford: Oxford University Press.

Cook, C. (2011) 'Fear of "race to the bottom" in education', *Financial Times*, 9 December. Retrieved from: https://on.ft.com/2ZWc8IQ

Coughlan, S. (2017) 'How Canada became an education superpower', *BBC News* [Online], 2 August. Retrieved from: www.bbc.in/3ct5exH

Department for Education (2010) *The importance of teaching.* London: The Stationery Office. Retrieved from: www.bit.ly/3doq6qV

Department for Education (2014) *The national curriculum in England: framework document.* London: The Stationery Office. Retrieved from: www.bit.ly/2ZQPAtc

Fordham, M. (2014) 'Assessment after levels: don't reinvent a square wheel', *Clio et cetera* [Blog], 29 October. Retrieved from: www.bit.ly/3gHJql6

Gibb, N. (2017) *The importance of an evidence-informed profession* [Address to Buckingham University PGCSE students]. Retrieved from: www.bit.ly/3co3Ega

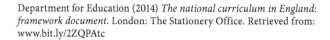
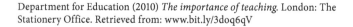

Gove, M. (2013) 'I refuse to surrender to the Marxist teachers hell-bent on destroying our schools: Education Secretary berates "the new enemies of promise" for opposing his plans', *Mail Online*, 23 March. Retrieved from: https://dailym.ai/2urH6LF

Government of British Columbia (2020a) *Curriculum overview.* Retrieved from: www.bit.ly/2yRpIlT

Government of British Columbia (2020b) *Core competencies.* Retrieved from: www.bit.ly/2yUKuB6

Government of British Columbia (2020c) *BC's new curriculum.* Retrieved from: www.bit.ly/2yS5x7p

Government of British Columbia (2020d) *BC's K–12 assessment system.* Retrieved from: www.bit.ly/3do2eUi

Government of British Columbia (2020e) *New curriculum info.* Retrieved from: www.bit.ly/3dma2Gn

Kilian, C. (2011) 'The last time we had an education commission', *The Tyee* [Online], 9 March. Retrieved from: www.bit.ly/3eGOBA3

Long, R. (2017) GCSE, *AS and A level reform (England).* London: The Stationery Office. Retrieved from: www.bit.ly/2Xkb4wH

Menzies, L. (2018) 'Making waves: maybe it's you who has the answer!', *The Centre for Education and Youth* [Blog], 14 September. Retrieved from: www.bit.ly/2ZWYuoU

Millard, W., Small, I. and Menzies, L. (2017) *Testing the water: how assessment can underpin, not undermine, great teaching.* London: Pearson/LKMco. Retrieved from: www.bit.ly/3cjI10B

Ofqual (2016) *Perceptions of A levels, GCSEs and other qualifications in England – wave 14.* Retrieved from: www.bit.ly/2MuUBjn

Ofqual (2017) *Perceptions of AS/A levels, GCSEs and other qualifications in England – wave 15.* Retrieved from: www.bit.ly/2XMv7Tz

Poet, H., Sharp, C., Garry, J., Harland, J., Keightley, G., Kirkup, C. and Martin, K. (2018) *Assessment without levels: qualitative research.* Department for Education. London: The Stationery Office. Retrieved from: www.bit.ly/3cmgfR5

Roberts, N. (2019) *The school curriculum in England.* London: The Stationery Office. Retrieved from: www.bit.ly/3clRLHG

Roberts, N. (2020) *Assessment and testing in primary education (England).* London: The Stationery Office. Retrieved from: www.bit.ly/3dq1r5w

Sanford, K. and Hopper, T. (2019) *Educational transformation: the BC story.* Victoria, BC: Houlihan Publishers.

Stacey, G. (2013) 'Our announcement on speaking and listening assessments', *The Ofqual Blog,* 4 September. Retrieved from: www.bit.ly/36QL8ME

Sullivan, B. M. (1988) *A legacy for learners: summary of findings.* Royal Commission on Education. Retrieved from: www.bit.ly/2XHelFi

Author bio-sketch:

Will Millard is head of engagement at The Centre for Education and Youth. He has undertaken research on a wide range of issues, and above all strives to ensure this research leads to action that will improve the lives of young people. A qualified teacher, Will began his career working in a large secondary school in North West London.

ASSESSMENT AND FEEDBACK AS PART OF A PROGRESSION MODEL

FREYA ODELL

A progression model

The introduction of a new Ofsted education inspection framework in 2019 has seen a renewed interest and focus on curriculum design, with Ofsted outlining their wish for a provider's curriculum to be 'coherently planned and sequenced towards cumulatively sufficient knowledge and skills for future learning and employment' (Ofsted, 2019a). Mary Myatt reinforces this point by stating that 'careful attention needs to be paid to the underlying knowledge which pupils need in order to access the subject in later years' (Myatt, 2018). Successful curriculum design, therefore, begins with identifying what knowledge and what skills are felt to be of greatest value to pupils, within subject domains, as they progress throughout the education system and into the world of work.

The role of assessment is critical to the curriculum design process. Whilst it is an evaluation of whether pupils have successfully acquired the knowledge and skills that we wish them to, determining what we assess and when is the first step in creating a successful progression model. Daisy Christodoulou argues that 'establishing an accurate and useful progression model is the foundation of any assessment system, because it explains how pupils make progress and what steps they need to take to get from one stage to the next' (Christodoulou, 2016). Establishing such a progression model is a complex task, however, if we are to consider knowledge acquisition, skill development and conceptual understanding.

Knowledge acquisition

Firstly, identifying what knowledge will support pupils in later years is key to the process of building a progression model. Charlie Pearson, head of English at St Joseph's Catholic School, teaches *Oliver Twist* in year 7 and gothic stories in year 8 as a precursor to the study of *A Christmas Carol* at GCSE. Whilst these choices are valid in themselves – being rich in description, using ambitious vocabulary and sentence structures, tackling key concepts and societal issues that are just as relevant today – by structuring her curriculum in this way, Pearson has established, developed and embedded knowledge about the Victorian era and the conventions of form within her pupils' long-term memory. This is helpful in reducing pupils' cognitive load when they start to study *A Christmas Carol* at GCSE as this background knowledge frees pupils' working memory up to focus on developing their knowledge of the narrative and other key components. Furthermore, in sequencing the curriculum in this way, pupils will be able to formulate links between the texts they study and gain a broader understanding of authorial intent during the Victorian era, creating a progression model that is both coherent and useful.

Skill development

Secondly, whilst acknowledging that skill acquisition sits within a bedrock of knowledge, the same attention needs to be given to the development of skills. When talking about the curriculum design process at Isaac Newton Academy, Rachel Macfarlane states the following:

> Heads of department, as the principal subject experts, would lead on the design of their curriculum, inspired by their vision of what knowledge and skills all students ought to learn and then working back from what would be required for study in that discipline at degree level, A level and GCSE. (2019)

A progression model should, therefore, consider what our best attaining students need to be able to demonstrate at A level/IB level and then plan backwards, establishing the incremental steps that pupils need to take in order to be able to confidently demonstrate that skill later on. For example, within English, IB students aiming for a grade 7 need to demonstrate that they can construct convincing and insightful and persuasive interpretations of the larger implications and subtleties of the text (International Baccalaureate, 2019). Consequently, our consideration when creating a progression model needs to be focused on how we support pupils to get to that point by identifying the steps that pupils need to take across the key stages – in this example, how we support pupils to develop the skill of interpretation.

Reading progression grid

	Y7	Y8	Y9	Y10	Y11	Y12-13
AO1 Read and understand a variety of texts, selecting and interpreting information, ideas and perspectives	I can identify and retrieve key details from a text. I can begin to make inferences and deductions. I can identify a writer's intention and viewpoint. I can support my ideas using relevant textual reference.	I can confidently infer meaning from a text. I can explain a writer's intention and viewpoint. I can draw upon well-chosen references to the text to support my ideas and explain these.	I can make a range of inferences and deductions. I can offer multiple interpretations of a writer's intention and viewpoint. I can select a range of relevant, focused evidence to support ideas.	I can demonstrate a thorough knowledge and sustained understanding of a text through a critical style. I can explore a writer's ideas and perspectives. I can select references that are detailed and fully support the points being and made.	I can demonstrate an assured knowledge and perceptive understanding of the text through a perceptive critical style. I can analyse a writer's ideas and perspectives. I can use apt and discriminating references to clarify the points being made.	I can demonstrate a thorough and perceptive understanding of the literal meaning of the text. I can construct convincing, insightful and persuasive interpretations of the larger implications and subtleties of the text. I can select the best quotations to effectively support the ideas being presented.
AO2 Understand and analyse how writers use linguistic and structural devices to achieve their effects	I can identify language and structure features and demonstrate an understanding of how they have been used to create an effect to show a broad understanding.	I can clearly explain how language and structure features are used to achieve an effect, including the use of vocabulary, sentence structures and other language features.	I can explore how a range of language and structure features are used to achieve effects, including the use of vocabulary, sentence structures and other language features.	I can demonstrate a thorough understanding and exploration of language and structure and how these are used to achieve effects, including the use of vocabulary, sentence structures and other language features.	I can demonstrate a perceptive understanding and analysis of language and structure and how these are used by writers to achieve effects, including use of vocabulary, sentence structure and other language features. I can evaluate the interrelationship of the language, form and structure used by the writer and their effect on the reader.	I can demonstrate a consistently insightful and convincing analysis of textual features and / or broader authorial choices. I can construct a very good evaluation of how such features and / or choices shape meaning.
AO3 Explore links and connections between writers' ideas and perspectives as well as how these are conveyed	I can make simple comparisons between two texts.	I can make developed comparisons between two texts.	I can make a range of specific comparisons between texts, including across different genres.	I can make a wide range of comparisons between texts.	I can make a varied and comprehensive range of comparisons between texts.	I can offer an insightful interpretation of the similarities and differences between the works.
AO4 Show understanding of the relationships between texts and the contexts in which they were written.	I can show an awareness of the relevant context with a simple comment on the relationship between text and context.	I can show an understanding of the context with a developed comment on the relationship between text and context.	I can show a developed understanding of context with analytical comments on the relationship between text and context.	I can demonstrate a detailed awareness of the relationship between text and context.	I can integrate an understanding of the relationship between text and context convincingly.	I can demonstrate a thorough and perceptive understanding of the relationship between text and context.

Progression grid English from KS3 to IGCSE to IB.

Conceptual understanding

According to Wiggins and McTighe (1998), a concept is 'a "big idea" – a principle or notion that is enduring, the significance of which goes beyond particular origins, subject matter or a place in time'. Conceptual understanding underpins the foundations of curriculum design within the International Baccalaureate Diploma Programme, with prescribed syllabi outlining how students may develop their conceptual understanding across the different key stages. The IB programme argues that

concepts have an essential place in the structure of knowledge. They require students to demonstrate levels of thinking that reach beyond facts or topics. Concepts are used to formulate the understandings that students should retain in the future; they become principles and generalisations that students can use to understand the world and to succeed in further study and in life beyond school. (Morris, 2009)

Furthermore, Erickson (2008) argues that using concepts

- creates connections to students' prior experience.
- brings relevance to student learning.

- facilitates deeper understanding of content knowledge.
- acts as a springboard for students to respond to their learning.

Concepts fall into two categories: key concepts and related concepts. Key concepts are 'broad, organizing powerful ideas that have relevance within and across subjects and disciplines' (Von Wrede-Jervis, 2019) (for example: culture, creativity, systems, time, place and space) whilst related concepts are domain specific. For example:

- English: character, setting, genre, audience imperatives
- History: chronology, cause and consequence, change and continuity
- Geography: place, space, environment, sustainability

Lois Lanning provides us with the example of character. She states that

> the concept of 'character' is highly abstract for a kindergartener. In response to the teacher's question, a child may correctly identify a particular character in a story (skill) but not understand 'character' as a concept. When teachers continue to provide rich examples of characters across many different types of texts, students begin to see conceptual patterns of the idea of 'character'. (Lanning, 2013)

Similarly, in a blog post on curriculum design, Claire Hill, an assistant headteacher in Kent, states, 'The first thing I would start with are the concepts I want students to understand and the texts that best lend themselves to exploring those concepts' (Hill, 2019). She went on to state:

> So, what do I know about my GCSE texts? I know that there are many allusions in *Macbeth* – both to mythology and biblical testament so I am going to include both in KS3 – perhaps when looking at Roman mythology and allusion. I know that there is a lot of phantasmagorical imagery in *Macbeth*. This form of imagery is rich for analysis, and I know it appears in *Alice in Wonderland*, which offers an opportunity to teach a canonical Victorian text as well … If I then take my thread of phantasmagorical imagery a little further, I can weave this into teaching war poetry in year 9 and *Jekyll and Hyde* in year 10. So, I have a good thread that takes me through year 7, 9 and 10 plus anything in between. This is clearly just one single thread, there are many more, but it is perhaps a good example of using threads (concepts) to weave through a curriculum to help create coherence and help me with my text choices. (Hill, 2019)

Summary

When we combine all three of these thought processes – the knowledge that we want our pupils to acquire, the skills we wish them to develop and the concepts we think are integral to our subject – the process of creating a progression model is complex. It requires careful thinking about what we value, how we sequence what we value, and the what, how and when of assessment to support pupils and prepare them for any 'future learning and employment'.

Formative assessment: breathing life into the progression model

If a progression model 'explains how pupils make progress and what steps they need to take to get from one stage to the next' (Christodoulou, 2016), then formative assessment is the enlivening of the progression model within the classroom. John Hattie defines formative assessment as the information we glean as teachers that '"closes the gap" between where a student is and where the student needs to be' (Hattie and Clark, 2019). Otherwise termed 'responsive teaching', when done well, formative assessment dramatically improves the progress of pupils (Black and Wiliam, 2005). The key being, as outlined in the Ofsted school inspection handbook, that 'teachers check pupils' understanding effectively, and identify and correct misunderstandings' and that 'teachers use assessment to check pupils' understanding in order to inform teaching' (Ofsted, 2019b).

Great formative assessment

From a teacher's perspective, great formative assessment is 'specific and focused' (Christodoulou, 2016) against a particular 'standard' (Hattie and Clarke, 2019) and 'in response to the qualities of the individual child's work. It is reflective on progress made' (Crooks, 2001) whilst providing feedback that is incremental and that will support pupils moving 'from their current state to the goal state' (Wiliam, 2018).

Yet formative assessment can only be effective when pupils actively engage with the process. In order for them to do so, we, as educators, must acknowledge that 'motivation and self-esteem are crucial influences on learning' (Black and Wiliam, 1998). To maintain pupil motivation and self-esteem, firstly, pupils need to understand the progression model, have the confidence to assess themselves and understand how to improve, and possess the awareness that deep learning occurs over time, with the feedback from formative assessment contributing to this. Secondly, pupils need to appreciate that errors are the norm and 'the key to new learning' so these should be celebrated and embraced, secure in the knowledge that everyone can improve.

Sequencing

Sequencing or stepped learning is an essential component of the progression model and helps to establish effective formative feedback because it enables feedback that is both focused and specific. Christodoulou (2016) states that 'if we want pupils to develop a certain skill, we have to break that skill down into its component parts and help pupils to acquire the underlying mental model'. For example, when teaching the skill of essay writing, there are several necessary steps to go through before the final product is completed. We might wish to consider how we

- create an effective introduction
- establish key arguments
- create strong topic sentences
- embed evidence
- conclude in an effective way

with each of these parts being taught across a sequence of lessons. And yet, we need to consider not only the steps we must take but also the order in which we teach these steps to scaffold pupils' learning. We would not teach how to write an effective introduction before we have established our key arguments and constructed strong topic sentences, for example.

Success criteria

Once the sequence of learning has been established, the learning intentions and success criteria, for each component part, can be written. According to the Gillingham Evaluation Study (Clarke, 2001, cited in Hattie and Clarke, 2019), it is the 'generation of clear, decontextualized success criteria that has a significant impact on learning' (Hattie and Clarke, 2019) with Hattie citing an effect size of 1.13. Susan Strachan, a head of English in Bristol, crafted the following success criteria to support her pupils in writing effective introductions (Strachan, 2018):

You will be successful when you

- are concise – use only 3–4 sentences for the introduction.
- remain focused on the question – use the key word within your opening sentence.
- use the writer's name.

- use adverbs to position yourself as an authority on the subject.
- contextualise the extract or provide a brief over of the story.
- use a rule of three or a list to introduce the events your will discuss in the essay.

In creating success criteria, like the above, not only are teachers equipped with a framework for effective formative assessment but pupils are provided with a clear understanding of the end goal and the steps they need to take in order to achieve that goal.

Yet for this to be most effective, Hattie and Clarke (2019) argue that 'the learner has to possess a concept of the standard (or goal or reference level) being aimed for'. Ensuring pupils see a range of examples of the 'goal' is significant in helping pupils to conceptualize what they are being asked to produce. As a result, Strachan (2018) illustrates what an effective introduction looks like, alongside her success criteria:

> Interestingly, Eric (the son of Mr and Mrs Birling) is presented by Priestley as fairly useless. The play charts the downfall of the family due to the appalling way they treat Eva Smith. Ironically, Eric seems most shaken by the Inspector's visit. He is seen as a lazy, thieving drunk, a womanizer and as a fairly pathetic character throughout the play.

Spending time deconstructing an example against the provided success criteria enables pupils to identify how the different components work together to create the end product, and fosters confidence ahead of pupils completing the task themselves, something which we know is integral to the learning process. In formatively assessing pupils' work, comparisons can then be made against the standard and the very specific success criteria with feedback focused on the criteria not met, in order to close any learning gaps.

Practice

Finally, once the sequence of learning has been established and clear learning intentions/success criteria written with the knowledge/skill taught, time needs to be given over to pupils to practise. Practice can take one of three forms – guided, deliberate or independent – and is reflective of a process such as learning to ride, where confidence is gradually gained, and support, such as the use of stabilizers, can be gradually removed.

Guided practice is where the teacher is involved in helping pupils put into practice what they've learnt and is often completed in groups. During the guided practice process, there is a greater level of interactivity between teachers and pupils, with assessment and feedback being more immediate and allowing for further opportunities to address misconceptions, offer positive or corrective feedback and, where necessary, re-model, re-explain and re-teach content. Tom Sherrington (2019) states that 'the practice must be guided so that the chance of forming misconceptions is minimized. Not only that: the guidance is key to generating the high success rate that in turn fuels motivations and engagement during independent work.'

In comparison, Daisy Christodoulou explores the idea of deliberate practice, introduced initially by Dr Engelmann through his instructional programmes. Christodoulou (2016) states that deliberate practice

> is based around the isolation and practice of the particular subskill one wants pupils to be able to do. In the case of the capital letter, the best approach would be to set up a series of activities that require pupils to use the capital letter correctly. For example, pupils might write out four or five simple sentences that use capitals correctly.

A common feature of practice is the repetition of a very specific skill which when mastered feeds into a more complex task.

The idea of what to practice comes into question when you consider Christodoulou's argument that 'the dominant generic skill model of instruction is based on the flawed premise that practising the final skill will improve the final skill. In actual fact, not only are such activities not the best way of developing the final skill, but in many cases they are actually counter-productive' (2016). This is something that Louisa Enstone, an English teacher from London, has been considering in her work with key stage 3. Enstone decided to move away from the traditional essay assessment structure with her year 7 class to focus in on creating a system that assessed smaller components of knowledge. She did this to give her pupils a more positive experience of assessment and to show them that what they knew about the text was also valued. An example of one such assessment is on the opposite page:

LO: Can I show my understanding of the ideas in *Hamlet*?

Part 1 – Remembering what you've learnt

1. Who are all of these characters? Explain their role and how they are related to the other characters. (1 mark per correct piece of information)

    - The ghost
    - Gertrude
    - Claudius
    - Hamlet
    - Fortinbras
    - Ophelia
    - Polonius

2. In your own words, explain what happens when Hamlet meets the ghost? (5marks)

    - Where and when did Hamlet see the ghost?
    - What different things does the ghost tell Hamlet?
    - How does Hamlet react to the ghost's message?

3. The ghost states: 'The serpent that did sting thy father's life now wears his crown.' What technique is used in this quote? (1 mark)

    A metaphor? ☐   Personification? ☐   A simile? ☐

4. How does Hamlet behave after his meeting with the ghost (to hide his thoughts and feelings)? (1 mark)

5. Hamlet gives a soliloquy that begins 'To be, or not to be: that is the question'. In your own words, what is Hamlet saying here? (1 mark)

6. Who is Hamlet speaking to when this 'Get thee to a nunnery: why wouldst thou be a breeder of sinners?' What does Hamlet mean? (2marks)

7. In your own words, explain what happens with Hamlet's play, The Mousetrap. (8 marks)

8. After The Mousetrap, Claudius goes to pray. He says:

    O, my offence is rank it smells to heaven;
    it hath the primal eldest curse upon't,
    Abrother's murder. Pray can I not.

    What does the underlined phrase mean? (2marks)

9. What happens in Gertrude's private rooms after the Mousetrap? (4 mraks)

10. What do you think will happen next? Explain your ideas. (3 marks)

This type of assessment offers opportunities for both guided practice (in terms of pupils' knowledge of the play) and deliberate practice – in being able to explain key quotations. And whilst Enstone has used this form of assessment instead of a conventional essay question, it would be an excellent way of practising 'sub-skills' and receiving feedback before applying what has been learnt to a more cognitively demanding task.

Formative assessment: the role of oracy

The most significant difference I have encountered in moving from the English education system to the international sector is the importance given to oracy, especially as a way of developing ideas and presenting an assimilation of learning. Mary Myatt (2018) argues that 'the development of talk underpins everything else: all learning, including reading and writing'. Below are some strategies I have encountered which use oracy as a tool.

ORACY TO DISCUSS AND STRENGTHEN IDEAS

1. **Think/pair/share** – a simple activity in which the teacher poses a question and asks pupils to consider the question individually during a period of silence before joining with another pupil to discuss their thoughts. This can be repeated in a group of four before the thoughts are shared with the whole class. A fantastic task for fostering confidence in pupils who are slightly more reticent to share as they will have run their ideas past other pupils first.

2. **Jigsaw** – Hattie states an effect size of 1.20 for the jigsaw activity. I have previously used this task to explore characterization in section 2 of *Of Mice and Men*. Pupils are organized into groups and each group is assigned a different character to explore within an allotted time, with a focus on appearance, behaviour and dialogue. After this time, pupils are re-organized into new groups made up of pupils who have been exploring different characters. Each pupil in the group is responsible for teaching the others about their character.

3. **Socratic discussions** – after studying a text, a small group of pupils form a Socratic circle. An open-ended question is assigned to the circle, which they have to discuss openly. As they are discussing, pupils around the outside think of ways in which they could **a)** add to, **b)** build on or **c)** challenge the discussion. At different points during the discussion, the inner circle are stopped and the outer circle can make their contributions. If their comment is valid, they can then swap with pupils in the inner circle.

4. **Live marking** – after the setting of a task – for example, a question analysing how a writer has used language and structure to present a viewpoint – two or three pieces of work are selected and placed under a visualizer to live mark, with the teacher explaining what is being rewarded and why. Two amazing things will happen: firstly, pupils will amend their own work as you are going through this process; and secondly, all pupils will want their work assessed under the visualizer. After you have marked a couple of pieces, pupils could have time to discuss their work with others to compare.

5. **Talk partners** – a lovely idea by Shirley Clarke. Each term, swap the seating plan of your class so that pupils have the opportunity to work with different pupils. A brilliant yet simple strategy for developing pupil confidence in having dialogues with a variety of different people.

The strategies above offer ways in which pupils can have the opportunity to discuss and share their ideas with their peers whilst you, as their teacher, can assess their knowledge and understanding in a formative way.

ORACY TO PRESENT ASSIMILATED LEARNING

However, oracy can also be used to present on learning as well. This is an area of strength within the Diploma Programme and the Italian education sector.

THE INDIVIDUAL ORAL

All pupils within the IB programme studying English language and literature A have to undertake an individual oral. This is where they have to select two texts – one literary and one non-literary – and comment on how effectively they present a global issue. It is completed in exam conditions, with minimal notes, and is recorded for examining purposes. This kind of assessment exposes students' understanding and thinking, whilst teaching students to be succinct in presenting their ideas. It is also good preparation for the future for when they attend job interviews or have to conduct presentations because it encourages them to consider the importance of oral literacy skills. And whilst an oral is not formally assessed in England any more, building in opportunities for pupils to present an assimilation of their learning is key, both to demonstrate their understanding and to foster confidence in articulating ideas. Within the international sector, it is a regular expectation that pupils will present their thinking and their ideas. For example, when reading a novel, I have assigned key passages and asked pupils to present an analysis of these (after having modelled the process myself). However, there is also scope in asking pupils to record their learning away from the classroom, if logistically this isn't a possibility. Pupils could be asked to record a commentary on a text, or complete a podcast or make a short YouTube video, which could then be shared and assessed.

TERZA MEDIA EXAM

The Italian sector also have an exam called the *terza media*. Part of this exam is an oral component in which Italian students have to present to a panel of teachers on a topic of their choosing which draws upon all of the disciplines studied. It is an intimidating exam but one in which pupils can showcase their learning from their key stage 3 schooling and is worthy of consideration. Having recently redrafted my key stage 3 long-term plans, in which each year group is governed by a key concept, I am going to create the opportunity for individual presentations at the end of the year with a focus on the key concept but which draw upon the learning from the different texts we have studied across the year. This is an excellent way for pupils to showcase their knowledge, skills and conceptual understanding whilst fostering their confidence in presenting to a wider audience.

References

Black, P. and Wiliam, D. (1998) 'Inside the black box: raising standards through classroom assessment', *Phi Delta Kappan* 80 (2) pp. 139–144.

Black, P. and Wiliam, D. (2005) *Inside the black box: raising standards through classroom assessment.* London: Granada Learning.

Christodoulou, D. (2016) *Making good progress? The future of assessment for learning.* Oxford: Oxford University Press.

Crooks, T. (2001) 'The validity of formative assessments', *Annual meeting of the British Educational Research Association.* University of Leeds, 13–15 September. Retrieved from: www.bit.ly/2zWQ32n

Erickson, H. L. (2008) *Stirring the head, heart and soul: redefining curriculum and instruction.* 3rd edn. Thousand Oaks, CA: Corwin Press.

Hattie, J. and Clarke, S. (2019) *Visible learning: feedback.* Abingdon: Routledge.

Hill, C. (2019) 'Curriculum as tapestry: a process for weaving together a curriculum', *A Classroom of One's Own* [Blog], 23 June. Retrieved from: www.bit.ly/2zZfe4h

International Baccalaureate (2019) *Language A: language and literature guide.* Cardiff: International Baccalaureate (UK). Retrieved from: www.bit.ly/2Xty50v

Lanning, L. (2013) *Designing a concept-based curriculum for English language arts: meeting the common core with intellectual integrity.* Thousand Oaks, CA: Corwin Press.

Macfarlane, R. (2019) 'A great secondary school curriculum' in Blatchford, R. (ed.) *The secondary curriculum leader's handbook.* Woodbridge. John Catt Educational, pp. 87–92.

Morris, I. (2009) *Teaching happiness and well-being in schools: learning to ride elephants.* London: Continuum International Publishing Group.

Myatt, M. (2018) *The curriculum: gallimaufry to coherence.* Woodbridge: John Catt Educational.

Ofsted (2019a) *The education inspection framework.* London: The Stationery Office. Retrieved from: www.bit.ly/2A3xBVj

Ofsted (2019b) *School inspection handbook.* London: The Stationery Office. Retrieved from: www.bit.ly/2MpnTzJ

Sherrington, T. (2019) *Rosenshine's principles in action.* Woodbridge: John Catt Educational.

Strachan, S. (2018) 'Why I love...essay introductions', *What I Love...* [Blog], 29 September. Retrieved from: www.bit.ly/2AE5yMQ

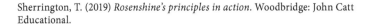

Von Wrede-Jervis, A. (2019) 'Transfer: building a conceptual and connected curriculum', *ManageBac* [Blog], 24 October. Retrieved from: www.bit.ly/2XWFrIL

Wiggins, G. and McTighe, J. (1998) *Understanding by design.* Alexandria, VA: Association for Supervision and Curriculum Development.

Wiliam, D. (2018) *Embedded formative assessment.* Bloomington, IN: Solution Tree Press.

Author bio-sketch:

Freya Odell has been teaching for 18 years. She has led on all key stages within English, been a director of English, head of faculty (line-leading MFL and humanities) and a director of learning. Freya is currently teaching English at St George's British International School in Rome and enjoying living *la dolce vita*.

HOW DOES ASSESSMENT SHAPE THE WAY WE TEACH ENGLISH AND MATHS?

KRIS BOULTON

There are two dominant assessment models: the **difficulty model** and the **quality model**. Mathematics exams are an example of a pure difficulty model, while English literature exams are an example of a pure quality model. Most of us aren't aware that these two models exist; they're not a part of our training, they're not talked about in schools, and they're not mentioned explicitly in the materials provided by the exam boards. This is surprising, and even worrying, since they dramatically shape not just the kinds of questions we pose in lessons, but also how we *conceive* of our subjects. Your own thoughts on what your job actually is – either to teach children what we know about science or to teach them to become practitioners of science themselves – will be heavily influenced by the assessment paradigm in use. Furthermore, the model in use is a matter of choice, not predetermined by the inherent nature of the subject. English could use a difficulty model, and mathematics could use a quality model.

So, what separates these two models, how do they impact us, and do we need to do something about it?

To answer those questions, we first need to look at what is inherently different between the subjects. We then need to understand the difference between what we call a 'subject' and what academics in universities call a 'discipline'. Finally, we'll look at the assessment models themselves and the impact they have.

Substantive content can have differing compositions

English and mathematics are two hugely different subjects to teach in school. They are commonly regarded as almost polar opposites. English is often thought to involve discussion and the expression of **novel thoughts** of one's **own**, while mathematics is often thought to involve the application of processes and reasoning that were **previously thought** by **other people**.

How we think of the English and maths subjects doesn't have to look this way, though. In the past, the English subject involved knowing (as Matthew Arnold put it) 'the best of what has been thought and said' . Today, you might be asked for your observations or analysis, and the idea that you read a book simply to know the book, and know what *others* think of it, including the author and their intent, would be misplaced in the English subject today. At the start of *Reading Reconsidered*, Doug Lemov notes that:

> In many schools, reading has come to be tacitly defined as 'the act of asking and answering questions about a text'. ... Seen historically, **the prioritization of how we read over what we read may be more divergence than norm**. ... The purpose of reading Paradise Lost as a student in the nineteenth century was probably at least as much that of being familiar with the story and being able to refer to it on the right occasion as it was to develop a unique and trenchant interpretation of it. The job was in **understanding Milton's purpose** of 'justify[ing] the ways of God to men' **more than it was in critiquing it**. [emphasis added] (Lemov et al., 2016, p. 18)

So, 'being good at English in school' could involve recalling from memory some facts about a piece of writing, quotes from the writing, what others have said about it, or succeeding in understanding the author's intent. This is entirely different from the common conception of 'being good at English in school', which means, for example, as the AQA (2018) mark scheme claims, being able to offer a 'critical, exploratory, well-structured argument'.

If we can conceive of the subjects differently, then does that mean English and maths lessons *could* look very similar? Probably not. Fundamentally, all school subjects are composed of **concepts, facts** and **cognitive** or **physical processes** that we want people in our society to possess, or to which we believe they should be entitled. Even if we reconceptualised English literature to prioritise recall, as described, it would be composed of an absolute smorgasbord of facts, some concepts, and very few (if any) processes. Conversely mathematics would still be composed of a great many processes, and many concepts, but relatively few facts.

So, there are very real and fundamental distinctions between the subjects and what we expect children to learn from them. However, there is also huge latitude in how we conceive of them, to the point that much of literature lessons from the past would be unrecognisable in today's classrooms.

Subjects are not disciplines

How does human civilisation advance its knowledge? Traditionally, the university was the institution for advancing human knowledge. Although today there are many avenues through which human knowledge is amassed (large private companies often have their own research divisions, for example), the university is an institution that has endured and continues to contribute an enormous portion of new human knowledge.

To organise themselves, universities formed 'academic disciplines'. If knowledge of a certain type could be defined, distinct from other types, then an academic discipline was formed to advance it. The discipline would have its members – people who seek to create new knowledge – and it would have its methods – the means by which its members created or acquired that new knowledge and assessed each other's propositions for their worth and admittance into the discipline.

From this, two *types* of knowledge can be defined within the universities: **substantive** and **disciplinary**. Substantive knowledge was the 'stuff' the academics sought out; it was knowledge of the past for history, and knowledge of nature for the sciences. Disciplinary knowledge included methods of research and investigation; the means of teasing out truth from the limited information available, coupled with human ingenuity.

School subjects are not academic disciplines. School pupils are not academics. Children in schools, and usually even young adults in universities, are not expanding the frontiers of human knowledge. However, most subjects in schools bear a resemblance to an academic discipline. English, science, mathematics and history all have their academic analogues in the university, as do drama, art and music.

So, when we define a school subject, we have choices to make: do we convey only the substantive knowledge of the analogous discipline, or only its disciplinary knowledge? Do we try to convey both? If so, in what ratio, and could we even perhaps transmit the substantive knowledge while having pupils engage in disciplinary activities – for example, could we have them learn Pythagoras' theorem by discovering it themselves in the process of conducting a mathematical investigation?

The choices we make affect the expectations we have for what students are to learn, and exactly how we expect them to perform when we assess their success in school, along with implications for how we assess them.

The difficulty and quality assessment models

There are broadly two modes of formal summative assessment in widespread use: the **difficulty** model of assessment and the **quality model** of assessment (Ahmed and Pollitt, 2002).

Difficulty assessment can be compared to the high jump (Ahmed and Pollitt, 2002) in the Olympic Games, where sportspeople are compared against one another by progressively raising the bar they have to jump over until they can no longer do it. Whoever clears the highest bar is the winner. Similarly, a difficulty-based assessment is composed of many relatively short questions which start easy and grow progressively more difficult as the pupil works their way through the exam paper (Ahmed and Pollitt, 2002). While pupils will usually miss a few questions here and there depending on which topics they most clearly remember on the day (or they'll pick up the odd mark from near the back of the paper) , the *design* of the exam paper is intended to rank pupils' performance based on how far they're able to progress through the paper – how high the bar can be raised until they can no longer clear it.

By contrast, a quality assessment model is what we see on our screens during an episode of *Strictly Come Dancing*. Someone comes out, offers a single performance, tries to perform well, and then someone judges them on the *quality* of that performance. To try to minimise 'rater error' – inaccuracy in the rating given by any one judge – multiple judges (four, in the case of *Strictly*) are assembled to each provide an independent judgement.

The AQA GCSE English Literature exam is an example of quality assessment in its purest form. Paper 1 from 2018 had only two questions, while paper 2 had only four questions to answer in total. There is no attempt to vary the difficulty between them; in fact, in paper 2 the pupil can select from 26 different questions to answer, if you include the various text choices. Options like this help the pupil pick which question they believe will be the easiest to respond to. The examiner's assessment is also heavily moderated: there are 'multiple judges'.

Conversely, the mathematics exam is an example of difficulty-based assessment in its purest form. Across three higher-tier examination papers in 2018, pupils were asked to respond to over 100 questions: 63 numbered questions, most with multiple sub-questions. Each paper began with questions that were intended to be easier and ended with questions that were intended to separate out the very highest-performing pupils; a mathematical high jump.

In the English exam, most questions were worth around 30 marks. In the maths exam, the highest scoring questions were typically only worth 5 marks, with one question being worth 6. It is a *choice* for these exams to be structured in this way. In the 1957 English Literature O level exam, developed by Cambridge Assessment, a candidate was asked to respond to five questions, with around 20 marks available for each question, and many of those had two to three sub-questions. Rather than one 'grand performance' worth 30 marks, the paper was split into a series of much smaller questions requiring shorter (but nevertheless demanding) responses. The paper has 32 available questions in total, so the candidate still has the opportunity to select which questions they prefer, but the questions are organised into the three sub-questions, which are of varying difficulty; this enables accessibility in a way that contemporary English literature papers do not. Many of the questions also stressed recall, as described in the first section of this chapter, 'Substantive content can have differing compositions'. Pupils were asked either to recall a standard cognitive process for translating Old English into Modern, or to recall facts and passages from texts they had read before the exam.

The assessments shape our teaching

To recap, academic disciplines are comprised of both **substantive** and **disciplinary** knowledge. In the analogous school subjects, we can choose to teach one or the other, or both. Then there are two dominant models of assessment, **difficulty** and **quality**, and for any subject we can choose to use either model.

What I now want to show is that this choice of assessment model has the most profound impact on how we conceive of both a school subject and its teaching. To do this, we're going to look at how English and mathematics, two subjects considered as distinct as possible from one another, would look very different from how they do today if their assessment models were changed. By the end, maths lessons might start to look a lot more like English lessons do today, and English, a lot more like maths.

Mathematics

First, mathematics. If mathematics used a quality model, the exam might have only four to six questions, each worth 30 to 50 marks. The only way to make sense of that is if the questions look very different from what we're used to. Currently, most questions are short, provide information about some simple situation, and then ask the student to apply a mathematical process to find some answer to the question, or respond correctly to an instruction (e.g. 'Solve this equation'). In a quality model, the question would instead have to involve students working on an extended problem, or undertaking a mathematical investigation, giving them the freedom to form and articulate their own conjecture and explore a simple premise as far as they choose in the time allowed. Their thoughts would have to be clearly documented, and they would be marked less for their ability to find a particular 'right answer' and more for the quality of their mathematical thinking and communication. In response, classroom teaching would probably change. Some concepts, facts and processes would still be taught as they would help students formulate their responses in the exam; but others, deemed less likely to be helpful, might be ignored.

From classroom to classroom, teachers would have significant scope to decide what concepts and processes they taught, just as English teachers today can choose to teach any of a huge range books. So, there would be some topics that probably everyone would still be taught (for example, solving linear equations and negative arithmetic), some topics that might become almost universally unfavourable (for example, shape transformations and pie charts), and others that might vary from classroom to classroom (like non-base-10 number systems). Since it would be less certain what aspects of mathematics pupils will have covered, the exam might even present several problems or investigations and give candidates a choice as to which they respond to, much like in the English exams. Effectively, the focus of maths lessons would likely shift from **communicating the substantive content** of mathematics to **the disciplinary content**. The lessons would become about trying to get pupils to think and behave like professional mathematicians, generating novel thoughts of their own, more than recalling and applying the thoughts that other people have had in the past.

English

Now, English. If English used a difficulty model, the exams would likely be composed of around 50 short-form questions, either closed response or multiple choice. The exam wouldn't ask pupils to produce writing or interpretations of their own any more. Instead, it would be testing whether or not they correctly comprehended the intended meaning of a passage. Individual multiple-choice questions can do this rigorously, and a battery of such questions can be designed to effectively eliminate the risk that someone scores well by chance alone (Zhao, 2006). Questions might expect pupils to have read poems and texts and be able to recall sections of them from memory, similar to the short-form questions in the 1957 O level paper mentioned above, and just as pupils in maths exams today are expected to be able to recall many concepts and processes. Lessons would likely shift from practising writing and expressing one's own thoughts to reading passages, memorising them, and identifying the 'correct' meaning of a passage, when presented with a choice. With this in mind, the prevailing attitude would have to shift from one where almost any analysis is treated as valid, provided it's well articulated and justified, to one where some perspectives are considered more valid than others. This would be quite a dramatic shift in educational philosophy (Marshall et al., 2018, p. 41).

Assessing understanding

Ahmed and Pollitt (2002) suggest that the **difficulty** model is appropriate for measuring **understanding**, while the **quality** model is appropriate for measuring performance in carrying out some activity. This suggests that – whether or not you consider it successful – school maths lessons today are focused on making sure school pupils understand mathematics, though not necessarily that they can act like mathematicians themselves. Conversely, English literature lessons are more focused on making sure pupils can perform a written critique or analysis, but not so focused on making sure pupils understand the content per se.

This might be surprising to anyone who thinks that an extended piece of writing, such as those asked for in the English exams, is an effective way of assessing someone's understanding. Surely that's a deeper and more rigorous assessment then a bunch of short-form questions? Well, consider all of the chance elements at play there. There are myriad parts in any piece of literature which pupils may or may not attend to in their response. The pieces of writing produced across the exams by so many pupils might work well enough for judging broadly who has better writing capabilities, but not so well for judging who has better understanding of various parts of the text. Each pupil must necessarily overlook so much in any one response, so you get no sense of what knowledge and understanding each pupil actually possesses, and no opportunity to directly compare a corpus of knowledge from one pupil to the next. You only get to observe what each of them has independently selected to present in that one moment. If you had in mind a particular understanding that you wanted to evaluate, there's no guarantee the pupil will choose to respond in a way that demonstrates it, and that will just be a consequence of their *choice*, not their knowledge.

Teaching paradigm

If the goal of your teaching is to ensure **understanding** of **substantive content**, then it is possible to do this with near perfect predictability and guaranteed success. Maths teachers might be perplexed and frustrated when pupils consistently forget content from earlier years, or fail to reproduce seemingly simple procedures, but under analysis these failings are almost invariably predictable, and a consequence of the pupils' educational experience to date. These issues can be eliminated entirely by changing the teaching that takes place in and across lessons (assuming behaviour isn't a barrier, of course). This model is **deterministic**. The inputs – the classroom teaching – inexorably lead to the desired outputs – understanding of **substantive** mathematical knowledge.

On the other hand, if your goal is to ensure **high-quality performance** of a **discipline's processes**, then it is only possible to increase the *probability* of success. The inputs will inevitably have to look different from the final output. Someone can improve their writing by reading more books, engaging in more academic conversations, increasing their vocabulary, and strengthening their command of grammar; and yet none of these things look like producing a piece of extended writing. The relationship is similar between input and final performance in competitive sport. The British cycling team in the 2012 Olympics attributed a portion of their dramatic success to things like sleeping on hypoallergenic pillows, a comfortable team bus, and even painting the floor white in the mechanics area of their team truck (Harrell, 2015). None of these activities look anything like high-performance competitive cycling, and yet they were all undertaken in the belief that they would have an impact on the final result. Feedback in English often follows a similarly probabilistic pattern. The incorrect use of a mathematical process can be corrected for next time. A poor piece of writing can only receive feedback relevant to *that* specific piece of writing, and it may or may not be helpful to some future piece. Increased performance comes as the cumulative effect of more and more feedback over time, but the relationship between all of these activities and the final product can only ever be probabilistic; no two pieces of writing will ever be identical.

Summary
The assessment model we choose can dramatically shape what happens in the classroom. This has three major consequences. It can shift the teaching and learning process from a focus on **substantive** knowledge to a focus on **disciplinary** knowledge ; it can shift it from a focus on **understanding** to a focus on **doing**; and it can shift it between a **deterministic** teaching paradigm and a **probabilistic** teaching paradigm.

The quality mode of assessment has produced an English classroom in which pupils are relentlessly asked for their own thoughts, rather than being asked for the thoughts of those who went before them, while the difficulty model of mathematics has left us with a world where no one understands how you can have a *job* as a mathematician – what do mathematicians *do*, other than answer questions all day? So, should we do something about this?

What can be done

As teachers, and especially as heads of departments and school leaders, we can choose our own internal assessment structures, which means they don't have to look like the national exams.

One friend of mine, an English teacher and deputy head, has told me he wants to build a suite of assessments for years 7–9 English that use the difficulty model only. His hope is that it will steer teachers towards asking pupils to memorise key facts and important details from works of literature and their historic context, as well as practising short grammar exercises. The GCSE exam will of course still focus on the quality of their written work, and if pupils produced no pieces of extended writing themselves until year 11, and received no feedback on their writing until then, they would likely perform very poorly. So, he intends to also ensure that pupils are asked to produce several pieces of extended writing each year, from which they will also receive formative feedback. Summative assessment, though, will focus on the new exams he's creating according to the difficulty model.

At a school I worked in, the head of department wanted to show pupils more of what it was like to work and think like a mathematician, so we created a series of extended investigations and problems for years 7–9. Each half term, they would be given one to work on, and then they would be assessed principally for the *quality* of what they handed in, including their approach and the clarity of their written communication. These would be completed in addition to our standard termly exams, which followed the usual difficulty model.

The benefit of a hybrid assessment model, like the two proposed above for English and maths, is that it ensures a pupil's experience in school covers the gamut of what's important: substantive knowledge *and* disciplinary knowledge; understanding *and* performance.

Unfortunately, change is hard in schools that already feel stretched beyond capacity. In my experience, we never got past the first half term. The exercise was a great one to introduce to the pupils, and the range of their responses was extensive; compared with what I would usually review, this was fascinating to see, and I've no doubt it would have revealed a very different side of mathematics to those pupils. But we didn't realise we were embarking on a quality model of assessment, didn't realise what we were doing paralleled the work of English teachers, and didn't realise that there was a lot we could have learned from them. I only had 23 pupils in key stage 3 at that time, while other teachers had over 60, but the time it took to mark and feed back on even just 23 pupils' work – especially when I'd never tried to assess work like this before and didn't really know what I was doing – meant I didn't get their work back to them for over two months. By that point, we should have been moving on to the second piece of work like this, but the head of department didn't mention it, and the rest of us didn't raise it, I think, because we all found it overwhelming to suddenly introduce such a paradigm shift into our classrooms .

Conclusion

First and foremost, be aware that these two models exist, and be aware of their impact. I have forever lamented the quality of my teacher training, and the more I've learnt about assessment and its influence, the more I've regretted that my teacher training never made it clear to me.

Second, know that the exams we use and the way they subtly direct us to conceive of our subjects is a *choice*. We can choose differently.

Third, and finally, it is possible to make that choice within the context of a school or department. If you want to go down that route, though, please do it with the awareness that you are introducing a paradigm shift, and asking teachers to engage in ways of thinking they've probably never had to before. You're also potentially asking teachers to increase their workload, if any new assessment is made *additional* to assessments you already have in place. Too much too soon, and your new system will quickly collapse. But a small change at first, increased over years, might move us slowly towards providing a fuller and more complete educational experience.

Bibliography

Ahmed, A. and Pollitt, A. (2002) 'The support model for interactive assessment', *IAEA Conference*, Hong Kong, 1–6 September. Retrieved from: www.bit.ly/2Ucp0al

AQA (2018) *English Literature: 8702/1 – paper 1: Shakespeare and the 19th-century novel* [Mark scheme]. Retrieved from: www.bit.ly/3cxeuk8

Harrell, E. (2015) 'How 1% performance improvements led to Olympic gold', *Harvard Business Review*, 30 October. Retrieved from: www.bit.ly/2YayAwA

Lemov, D., Driggs, C. and Woolway, E. (2016) *Reading reconsidered* [Ebook]. Hobokon, NJ: Wiley, pp. 17–18.

Marshall, B., Gibbons, S., Hayward, L. and Spencer, E. (2018) *Policy, belief and practice in the secondary English classroom: a case-study approach from Canada, England and Scotland.* London: Bloomsbury Publishing.

University of Cambridge Local Examinations Syndicate (1957) *Report on the work in English Literature, first alternative.* Cambridge: Cambridge University Press. Retrieved from: www.bit.ly/2Mxj5Io

Zhao, Y. (2006) 'How to design and interpret a multiple-choice-question test: a probabilistic approach', *International Journal of Engaging Education* 22 (6) pp. 1281–1286.

Author bio-sketch:

Kris Boulton is an international teacher trainer and education writer. He spent five years working as a maths teacher in inner-city schools and was an associate tutor and director at Teach First. He is currently director of education at Up Learn, an online platform that provides A level study and revision courses powered by cognitive science and AI.

AUTHENTIC ASSESSMENT
TOM SHERRINGTON

Introduction

How am I doing? Am I doing it right? How could I do better? What have I achieved? How good are my achievements?

These are some of the questions assessment is trying to answer. The central argument in this chapter is that assessment is at its most powerful – most effective at answering these questions – when the information generated and shared is authentic, rooted in concrete ideas about what students know rather than a series of artificial constructs.

Given that learning endeavours and subject disciplines vary significantly in the nature of the knowledge, skills and understanding that they represent, it is important for assessment information to reflect and respect that disciplinary variance if it is to be meaningful. Authentic assessment allows teachers and students and other interested parties, such as parents and leaders, to engage in conversations about learning using information that contains maximum meaning relative to the discipline.

Inauthentic assessment?

Problematically, the current practice in many contexts demands that teachers morph their assessment information into a form dictated by the perceived need for a uniform language around standards and notions of progress across all disciplines. Although this has some benefits at a certain level, as we will explore, where centralised system-needs dominate, a great deal of meaning can be lost from the information; it becomes inauthentic and, consequently, does not serve the purposes it was originally designed for.

How does **inauthentic assessment** manifest itself? Let's look at a reasonably common example encapsulating several problems this essay is trying to address.

Sara's half term report contains a set of numerical grades from her most recent assessment across all subjects. Each grade is based on the last seven weeks of school and the mandatory assessment set at the end of that period. She is in year 8 but 'GCSE-style' 9–1 grades have been adopted for ease of communication in all subjects. They are labelled 'working at' grades.

- Her 5 in English is for some extended writing; originally a 'band 2' that became 12/30 marks.
- Her 4 in science comes from scoring 33/60 on a one-hour science test on 'everything we've done so far'.
- Other grades started life as 17/30 on her geography assessment and 58% for her maths test.
- Her history grade is linked to a set of descriptors: 'Her 5 suggests she is "beginning to develop a secure understanding" whereas a 6 would have been "is developing a secure understanding".'
- Her art and music teacher, after six one-hour lessons, gave 'impressionistic' 'holistic' grades.
- Her French grade began as a hierarchical set of numerically graded 'can do' statements (e.g. 'Sara can use the past tense in describing her last holiday').

The 9–1 grades are logged onto a flight-path tracker. Her target grades are written on the front of her book and her teachers are required to plot these assessments on a graph to show if she is 'on track', 'exceeding' or 'below', relative to the line showing 'expected progress'.

Sara's attitude to learning grades are awarded on an A–E scale. She doesn't understand why she has B in English ('everyone gets a B') when mostly she gets As and has never had any complaints. The C in art seems anomalous.

Sara's books contain numerous 'verbal feedback given' stamps – 'proving' that the teachers gave feedback – and there are numerous 'can do' checklists stuck in her books.

- 'I can state that water is a liquid at room temperature.'
- 'I can list the advantages and disadvantages of a wind farm.'
- 'I know the difference between a simile and a metaphor.'

What does this assessment information tell Sara? How useful is this set of apparently standard-model grades to Sara, her teachers and her parents? Do they know how well she is doing and how she can improve? Is she really doing better in English than in science? Has it been helpful for the information to be uniform, so that there is a sense of consistency and a common language? Or, would it have been better to keep the information in the form it was generated in despite the apparent complexity? If we reported the scores, bands and percentages in a mixed form, would that be better? Even here, do we have a sense of what Sara actually knows she can do – the raw details of her work and performances that underpin the ticks, comments, scores and grades? And does the attitude to learning B in English say more about the teacher than it does about Sara? How would we know? What is she supposed to do differently?

The information raises lots of questions, largely because so much of it is inauthentic; most of it consists of abstractions and constructs that are far removed from any specific information that Sara can act on.

What are the purposes of assessment?

Various sources seek to define the purposes of assessment . It's instructive to explore. For example, when assessing 'success' in completing a physical journey, there is a formative process that is important. At multiple points – if not continuously – we need to know where we are; ideally we need some absolute sense of our position. We also need to know the destination – a goal of some kind, or multiple possible goals. It is by comparing our current position with the destination that we can plot our course and plan our immediate next steps.

Linked to this is a sense of standards. Are we doing well? This is different to the absolute position. We need to know if we are as far along the journey as we should be if we are going to consider ourselves – or be judged by others – to have truly succeeded (e.g. 'arriving in good time'). This quality judgement affects our motivation and effort in relation to completing the journey. There is also a summative element: once the journey is over, we can review how well it went in terms of both reaching the goal and how well we did so, either compared to previous attempts or the performance of others. We might use journey time as an indicator, in relation to a notion of the difficulty associated with making the journey.

Essentially, there are three interrelated elements, each of which has a formative and summative aspect. This can be a frame through which we can review the nature and value of assessments.

Assessment information	Formative	Summative
Absolute position	A concrete measure of learning; things that are known, understood or can be performed at a point in time	The final position reached
Goal distance	A measure of the gap remaining in what still needs to be known/ understood/performed compared to a defined set of goals	The final extent of learning relative to the defined set of goals
Quality judgement The standard	The current position compared to expected standards as determined by the cohort – 'How good is it?'	The final position compared to expected standards as determined by the cohort – 'How good was it?'

Many of the problems that arise, leading away from authentic assessment, stem from **confusing these different elements** both **within and across disciplines**. In reality, different forms of learning present significant inherent barriers to delivering meaningful information for some of these aspects. It's also important to consider, in parallel, where the information we generate goes next as this influences our thinking about the information we gather. Both formative and summative assessments can feed into a range of different processes:

Assessment process	Formative	Summative
Technical feedback a) to learner b) to teacher	Details of knowledge/degree of fluency secured and remaining gaps, metacognitive barriers	No inherent technical feedback unless used formatively
Motivation and self-regulation	Emotional response in terms of applying more/less effort and raising/ lowering goals; knowledge of self in terms of learning strategies and task/ goal management	Performance relative to goals or to others triggers motivational and goal-setting response, up or down, as with formative
Status and exchange	Informal 'status' value – with peers, in influencing teacher expectations and within a school community	Formal status value and material value in relation to progression routes and, ultimately, access to employment Aggregated to school-level status in community and accountability system

Authentic assessment happens when the information collected for a specific area of learning aligns with the process that it feeds into without losing meaning or, at the very least, without preventing that process from having a positive impact on learning. The issue with inauthentic assessment is that these assessment forms and the processes they support become entangled – and this happens in different ways for different curriculum areas, creating various problems.

The absolute-relative problem

One aspect of this is where we assume that grading can tell us about absolute position – but it can't. Grading is very explicitly a relative measure. There is no 'grade 6 position' per se; it's only meaningful as a comparison to how everyone else is doing and is only formally defined (by examination boards or large-scale comparative systems) in relation to terminal summative assessments taken by large cohorts.

The reverse aspect is the assumption that ungraded measures are absolute and can be considered to represent standards in their own right; actually they nearly always only have meaning when compared to the cohort as relative measures. We treat positional assessment information as if the standards are implicit or irrelevant.

How well am I doing? Is 65% a good score? Is a high jump of 1.07 metres a good jump? Well, that depends on you, but it also depends on the pattern of how other people are doing too. The score or height could be exceptional, average or terrible. Some people struggle to accept that this comparative element is almost always an inherent feature of assessment in terms of standards and value; it jars with people's aversion to creating the appearance of winners and losers which has motivational consequences in all directions.

A great non-educational example is the growth charts for babies.[11] If a baby is 65 cm long, head to toe, what does that tell you? On the face of it, this is an absolute measure – and yet, nobody ever tells you their baby's length. A quick study of the growth charts will tell you why. At three months, 65 cm is the 95th percentile for boys. This is 'huge' – the top 5% of all baby boys. But, by seven months, 65 cm is 'tiny' – the bottom 5%. So, given how rapidly the changes occur, the measure only has meaning in relation to the population. As a result, parents are more likely to report the percentile than the size because it has more meaning. Baby birth weight only has currency because it is taken at exactly the same point in time for all babies – so we learn the meaning of the scale; that 5 lbs is very low and 10 lbs is very high. By three months, we're back into percentile territory for meaningful discussions.

In terms of learning, some subjects can produce measures based on details of what students know and can do. There are very few areas with actual concrete

---

11.   US Centers for Disease Control and Prevention baby growth chart for boys – www. bit.ly/3eVD2VQ

measures: physical measures in sport (times and distances) and maybe reading speed and accuracy. More generally, we create scales by awarding marks for specific responses and count them up as assessment scores. Here we can track back to the granular information to support feedback when we need to. However, we still need to create meaning in terms of standards and goal distance. This leads us to construct judgement information by comparing performances.

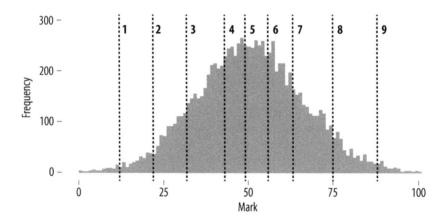

This is how grading of examinations works (Pointer, 2014). In this example from the trial GCSEs in 2014, scores on a maths test taken by several thousand students are scaled to range from 0–100. Clearly, the graph shows the classic bell-curve distribution. This curve isn't imposed on the data; the data takes this shape because, in common with numerous characteristics or fields of performance, most people in a population are broadly similar; they are grouped close to the average. Measures tend to be much less frequent the further from the mean we go – creating the bell shape. The shape of the curve is an inherent characteristic of the data – so it is possible to see where any student's score fits compared to the others. The question is how to communicate this. We could tell students their scaled score and, if we all knew that 50 was the scaled mean, we would immediately know something about the relative performance – and hence the standard. For reasons rooted in precedent and tradition and the quality-difficulty problem explored below, we've tended not to use scaled scores, opting instead for grading.

Crucially, it is important to be forever mindful that grading is entirely artificial. The number of grades and the score boundaries for each grade have no inherent meaning in relation to the material or the range of scores. They are constructs designed to communicate value and standards in a common language.

In GCSE exams, we can compare large-scale grade distributions between different disciplines. The curves are not the same (Stubbs, 2019). Proportionally more students gain higher grades in English Literature than in Maths and the mean is higher. This could be a feature of the subjects but is probably largely because the cohorts are not the same.

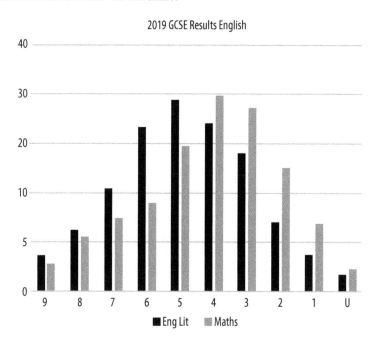

The problem arises at school level when we do not have large cohorts as a reference point or anything close to standardised assessments. Within a subject, there is huge variation and complexity inherent in test design, and yet teachers will convince themselves that they know that their small-scale unmoderated test scores can be equated to grades defined for national cohort terminal exams.

Worse still is when teachers treat the grades as a ladder: we begin at 3, then move to 4, then to 5, then 6. Some commercial tracker products even encourage users to decimalise this data: 4.4, 4.5, 4.6, etc. These 'fine grades' are created by teacher judgements linked to statement banks or test scores that have absolutely no connection to the boundaries generated for the terminal exams; they are a pure fabrication to create an illusion of precision and step-by-step progression that isn't meaningfully definable. There is no '4.5' grade in a subject that is definably distinct from '4.6' in terms of any set of knowledge and understanding in that subject. A GCSE grade is only meaningful at the end; until then, any grade generated from an assessment is merely a teacher's projection of what that grade might be in the future. Some questions are more difficult than others, but any attempt to grade questions is artificial. It's a ballpark notion at best; there is definitely no neat grade ladder of difficulty.

With no meaningful ladder, there is also no meaningful flight path. Countless systems use an imagined linear route from a starting grade (determined by a student's baseline performance in other tests – like the English SATs in year 6) to a final grade along which students should travel. These have been soundly debunked and exposed for their self-referential circularity and meaninglessness by Matthew Benyohai (2018), amongst others. Again, the illusion of progress from one absolute position to another is created when none of the points are more than artificially imagined positions on a bell curve; the default assumption being that students keep their place in the rank order.

Meanwhile, raw test scores have an authenticity in their own right. Sara's 17/30 score is an authentic measure. It is what it is. If Sara and her teachers know what she got right and wrong, that will help her improve. Perhaps telling her the class average will let her know how well she did compared to others, to put her performance in context, adding the quality judgement element, supporting her motivation to improve.

Authenticity check
➔ Don't grade individual short-answer questions.
➔ Don't use flight paths.
➔ Don't call interim grades 'working at' grades.
➔ Don't use 'GCSE-style' grades as a ladder.

The quality-difficulty problem
Here the issue is that insufficient attention is given to the different origins of assessment information with different relationships to grades and marks. Quality model (Christodoulou, 2016) assessments derive from judgements from

comparisons[12] forming an approximate continuum with notional gradations with which marks might be associated; difficulty model assessments generate marks that then aggregate into totals from which grades are constructed. Assuming equivalence across these different processes is problematic, especially with school-sized cohorts.

In a difficulty model subject, we build up. How many marks do we award for questions? Which combination of questions makes a good test of the material in hand? Some tests are easier than others; some generate wider distributions than others. Even in, say, year 8 maths, a series of tests out of 30 marks or 100 marks (i.e. a percentage) will vary in their mean and range. Any attempt to extrapolate from these marks to a standard grade would be based on a range of subjective judgements including the weighting of each contributing assessment.

Meanwhile, in a quality model subject, the teachers typically have a series of pieces of extended writing or a portfolio of products or performances to evaluate. Here the grading sense might precede the award of marks.

Typically, essay marking begins with a banding process – as few as three or four bands across the range. Once in a band, teachers fine-tune their judgements to arrive at marks. A drama teacher might have a sense of what a B looks like – a holistic judgement based on assessment experience – that is more coherent than their sense of how many marks to award. We might agree an essay fits within a broad standard but there is no 'true mark'. It is a matter of judgement that varies from marker to marker, within a range, even where extensive moderation takes place. Two markers might largely agree on the rank order of a set of assessments and yet disagree about the allocation of marks and where the grade boundaries might fall.

When the grades-to-marks or marks-to-grades approaches vary in their origin, the school-level validity in the award of a grade 5 in English and a grade 5 in maths is such that the grades themselves can't really be compared. We can't know that they represent the same standard. Similarly we can't know that a grade 6 in history represents 'better performance' than a grade 5 in geography. It's hard enough for exam boards with large-scale data to arrive at these comparisons, never mind doing it in schools with cohorts of 100 students. Even if every history teacher agrees, it's largely a matter of hope that the moderation

---

12. See the comparative judgement concept explained superbly on the nomoremarking.com website.

processes in history line up with those in geography to yield meaningful comparisons. And so, in reporting these grades to students and parents, we are essentially giving false inauthentic information.

To take the earlier Maths GCSE example, a grade doesn't tell us anything about the curriculum or knowledge content that underpins the standard. Arguably an experienced examiner or maths teacher would have a good overall sense of the typical knowledge that a student might have (and not have) based on the typical pattern of success with certain question types. But even they couldn't apply that to any one student. Even if we know the mark on the test, it doesn't immediately tell us what they got right and wrong unless we look at the paper. So grades and scores in isolation lose the granularity we need to provide feedback. They are essentially useless for that purpose – something that Dylan Wiliam and Paul Black explore in relation to marking grades and comments in *Inside the Black Box* (Black and Wiliam, 2005).

Grade-style information is non unimportant; we need it for motivation and value purposes. Grades serve as broad indicators of the standard; they provide a broad sense of quality which might inform our sense of the distance left to run. However, if a grade 6 originates from a raw score of 45/70 on a test, then we need clarity around how and why we use all of that information. Side by side, the two measures reinforce each other's meaning; but if the 6 is all anyone sees, most of the information has gone. Given all the issues with the 'ladder illusion' and the quality-difficulty problem, it is arguably more authentic to avoid grades altogether. There are other ways to contextualise a score, including providing class averages or box plots that show the spread.

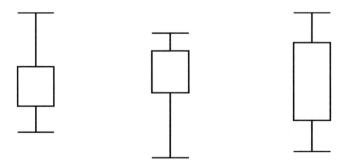

The box plots allow different profiles of scores to be compared in a complex way and allow any individual score to be put in context in more detail than simply comparing to the average.

In feedback terms, 45/70 suggests there are 25 marks' worth of errors to explore. Here, there's another level of decision-making about the nature of that feedback. Adam Boxer (2019) has made an excellent case that teachers serve students better not by dwelling on the specific errors in any formative exam, but by re-teaching the general underlying concepts and misconceptions that these errors suggest.

Authenticity check
→ Don't use universally constructed grades.
→ Don't use grades in isolation from their original raw-score form.
→ Consider using non-grade mechanisms to reference cohort performance: average scores and ranges or plots of raw scores.

The granularity problem
This refers to the practical and technical reality that feedback requires information that is granular if it is to be understood and acted upon in order to secure deeper learning and improved performance. However, often goal distance or standards information is most often conveyed in broader terms using scores or grades where the granularity is implied, masked or lost completely. Conversely, the volume of granular information available is vast and can't be readily communicated, except in a very dynamic, piece-by-piece fashion.

A key element of technical feedback in every curriculum area is finely granular. It consists of the minutiae of elements of knowledge and understanding: a brush-stroke in art; a precise movement in sport or music; a word in English; a symbol on a diagram or the label on an axis; the meaning or the sound of a word or the order of a set of events or steps. To generate this feedback, we need granular assessment tools, deeply embedded in the fabric of a specific curriculum, that can pick up the detail. We want them to do the job of locating our absolute position.

In reality, the greatest source of this kind of information will be verbal feedback – given individually or to a whole class; it's live, dynamic, in-the-moment formative assessment that has no scale or score and can't be recorded meaningfully; it's the everyday dialogue of student-teacher interactions and formative checking processes that run throughout every minute of the school day. Dylan Wiliam argues that this is the type of feedback that has the greatest impact on student learning.

Importantly, we usually need goal-distance information at the same moment as knowing our position so that we know what to do next. As Shimam ura discusses in his fabulous *MARGE* paper (Shimamura, 2018), cognitively, we tend to cease applying effort, marshalling the appropriate resources in our brains, if we think that we've achieved a goal of knowing something. We need to evaluate our knowledge against some external reference in order to determine whether we still have work to do. For example, if we're satisfied that we can match the names of a set of actors to their faces when both elements, faces and names, are presented to us, we understretch ourselves compared to a task requiring us to generatively recall the names of those same actors when only presented with their faces.

Goal-distance information is central to the mechanisms of self-regulation and generating positive motivation to engage in learning. As Wiliam reports, DeNisi showed how fraught this can be in terms of our response to goal-distance feedback. For some, if the distance is too great, they give up. For others, if the goal is easily reachable with minimal effort, they can reduce their effort, rather than set more ambitious goals. However we might respond, motivation to push ahead stems from giving value to a learning goal and working out how to get to it. Assessment information needs to inform this whole process. Again, the nature of that information is highly granular and curriculum-specific.

A key ingredient in a learner's goal-setting process and their response to the challenge is this idea of value; that the goal matters or constitutes success in some way. Often people want these things to be absolute – because then we can have a system and assessment culture where individual successes are independent of the successes of others; everyone can succeed in their own terms. In reality, that doesn't work in many cases, so we also need quality judgement information.

Relative quality assessment needs to reference the achievements of others and usually can't be done in practical or meaningful ways with fine-grained information; typically we need a wider sampling of knowledge and understanding to make that kind of comparative assessment. For example, when we compare two paintings, we can't compare them stroke for stroke; we have to look at the overall effect of many strokes for the comparison to have meaning; the same is true for samples of writing. In quality model subjects, we need exemplars to represent the standards. Exemplars of writing, products, portfolios – at the highest levels expected and at intermediate levels so that a path through the standards can be seen.

Reference exemplars

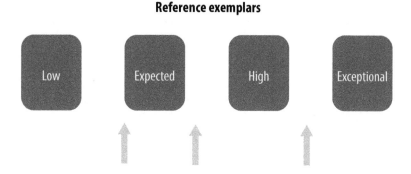

The standard of any given piece of work is defined in relation to a set of exemplars that represent a benchmark for comparison at different levels.

For difficulty model subjects, we need a sense of the total knowledge or terminal difficulty level expected, so that we can see how close we are to securing it for ourselves and compared to others. For example, in maths, we can see a range of questions at different difficulty levels as a reference for the point we've reached in our understanding.

Of course, beyond the self-regulation and motivational aspect in the learning process itself, it's this comparative dimension that forms the basis of the exchange value in terms of kudos and qualifications. The problem arises if we lose or devalue the granular information. If we only present students with standards information, they have nothing to use to move themselves forward.

Sometimes, schools try to tackle this issue in inauthentic ways, either generating unwieldy statement banks, listing all the knowledge students should have in fine detail, or generating tortured semantic hierarchies to establish some kind of scale of understanding – as in Sara's history report. The example given is from a real school:

> Her 5 suggests she is 'beginning to develop a secure understanding' of colonialism whereas a 6 would have been 'is developing a secure understanding' of colonialism.

It's meaningless to nearly anyone except the person writing those statements. Far better to set a test on the knowledge and writing skill associated with exploring the topic of colonialism and record and report the outcome in terms of raw marks for factual knowledge and/or an approximate band for any extended writing; this is authentic. Then provide Sara with granular feedback about the specific conceptual or factual gaps she needs to work on. That too is authentic.

Authenticity check
→ Don't use nebulous descriptors with semantic scales of difficulty.
→ Don't try to record everything a student knows on a tracker; it's too much data.

The fluidity problem
Our final problem is the fact that notions of success are not static or easily pinned down in absolute terms. If I can recall a fact in response to a direct question today (e.g. what is 13 squared? It's 169), does that mean I know it? What if I was only just told it the day before – do I still know it a month later, when the 'recency' effect has gone? (McCourt, 2019) Do I still know it if this fact is required without any prompting – recognising that 169 is 13 squared in a larger problem without the direct question to cue my recall? (McCourt, 2019) Can I recognise why 13 squared fits with a 5-12-13 triangle as the sum of 5 squared and 12 squared? (i.e. as an example of Pythagoras' theorem) What does it mean to 'know' anything when there is almost always a question of the degree of depth and fluency; there is always further deepening and maturation to come?

This applies to all of the examples in Sara's report

- 'I can state that water is a liquid at room temperature.'
- 'I can list the advantages and disadvantages of a wind farm.'
- 'I know the difference between a simile and a metaphor.'

With each example we can imagine the challenge of recency and cue, distorting the reliability of the assessment. More importantly, none of these statements puts the knowledge into a context of varying difficulty. How, for example, do we explain evaporation at room temperature? When listing an advantage of a wind farm, how far can Sara go in exploring environmental and economic factors – or is it just a case of knowing the names of factors without being to explain them? Can she provide a concrete example of metaphor or recognise one in Ted Hughes's 'Bayonet Charge' without prompting?

For any attempt to pin down 'can do', there are further questions of breadth and depth that render the simple tick effectively meaningless. Again, far better to set a test on a range of material relating to each of these areas, with questions spanning a range of difficulty, and then count up the marks. The marks will indicate a sense of absolute position if the test is focused on a tight set of knowledge; it will also provide goal-distance information if full marks were not achieved – and, if we know how everyone else did on average, we can know where Sara sits in terms of standards.

Authenticity check

→ Don't do 'can do' statements. Use tests and scores instead.

→ Avoid recency and cue by using a mixture of focused assessments and more synoptic assessments to get a better measure of learning successes.

→ Don't place excessive weight on one assessment; absorb the inherent fluctuations in test performance and difficulty by using multiple assessments to triangulate from .

Authentic assessment systems

As a conclusion, I am pleased to say that, increasingly, I see teachers and school leaders responding to the challenge of authenticity and putting assessment systems in place that support the ideas presented here. In general, they have the following characteristics:

- Leaders can talk the language of assessment as it applies to the specific needs of each subject; they learn how assessment works in different ways rather than seek to impose a centralised model.
- Teacher's mark books with messy columns of various data sets and shared departmental assessment records have authority and status over the centrally collated data system.
- There are no spurious flight paths; no 'can do' statements or unwieldy statement trackers. Reports to parents contain only things that are true, not things that are constructed to look true. Scores are presented and explained rather than morphed into grades.
- There is no rigid high-frequency, universal assessment timeframe imposed across all subjects; assessments happen when they naturally fall as determined by the curriculum, not the other way around.
- Central data is minimal – collected twice or at most three times a year. A rigid six-week regime is unlikely to support an authentic approach and this is less and less common.
- Reports contain raw scores and a form of cohort referencing or teacher comment, ideally not GCSE-style grades unless these are

explicitly defined as approximate cohort positions rather than implying they are tightly moderated positional measures.

- No GCSE-style 'working-at' grades and ladders exist, especially in the years far from the final examinations.
- Instead of subjective comments about student attributes and attitudes, the reports indicate objective concrete actions a student should take to improve.

References

Benyohai, M. (2018) 'The difference between measuring progress and attainment', *Medium* [Website], 7 June. Retrieved from: www.bit.ly/30d8pH8

Black, P. and Wiliam, D. (2005) *Inside the black box: raising standards through classroom assessment.* London: Granada Learning.

Boxer, A. (2019) 'What to do after a mock? Assessment, sampling, inferences and more', *A Chemical Orthodoxy* [Blog], 26 March. Retrieved from: www.bit.ly/2ALlDQw

Christodoulou, D. (2016) *Making good progress? The future of assessment for learning.* Oxford: Oxford University Press.

McCourt, M. (2019) *Teaching for mastery.* Woodbridge: John Catt Educational.

Pointer, W. (2014) *Setting the grade standards in the first year of the new GCSEs.* Manchester: AQA Centre for Education Research and Practice. Retrieved from: www.bit.ly/2ADseg2

Shimamura, A (2018) *MARGE: a whole-brain learning approach for students and teachers.* Scotts Valley, CA: CreateSpace Independent Publishing Platform.

Stubbs, B. (2019) 'National percentage figures for GCSE grades', *Student Performance Analysis* [Website]. Retrieved from: www.bit.ly/3gWiBK3

Wiliam, D. (2011) *Embedded formative assessment: practical strategies and tools for K–12 teachers.* Bloomington, IN: Solution Tree.

Author bio-sketch:

Tom Sherrington is an education consultant and author. He writes the popular blog teacherhead.com and his books include *The Learning Rainforest* and best-seller *Rosenshine's Principles in Action*. With 30 years' experience as a physics and maths teacher and school leader, including 11 years as a headteacher, Tom is now in demand from schools across the UK and around the world to deliver CPD for teachers and leadership teams. He works with several schools and colleges providing consultancy support on curriculum and improving the quality of teaching. He is a regular keynote speaker and contributor to conferences and education festivals.